△ The Triangle Papers: 58

The NEW CHALLENGES TO INTERNATIONAL, NATIONAL AND HUMAN SECURITY POLICY

A Report to
The Trilateral Commission

Authors: ANNE-MARIE SLAUGHTER
Dean, Woodrow Wilson School of Public and
International Affairs, Princeton University

CARL BILDT
Chairman, Nordic Venture Network and
Senior Advisor, IT Provider

KAZUO OGURA
President, The Japan Foundation

D1072727

published by
The Trilateral Commission
Washington, Paris, Tokyo
2004

THE TRILATERAL COMMISSION

www.trilateral.org

1156 15th Street, NW
Washington, DC 20005

5, rue de Téhéran
75008 Paris, France

Japan Center for
International Exchange
4-9-17 Minami-Azabu
Minato-ku
Tokyo 16, Japan

THE AUTHORS

ANNE-MARIE SLAUGHTER is Dean of the Woodrow Wilson School of Public and International Affairs and the Bert G. Kerstetter '66 University Professor of Politics and International Affairs at Princeton University. She served as President of the American Society of International Law from 2002 to 2004. Prior to becoming Dean, she was the J. Sinclair Armstrong Professor of International, Foreign and Comparative Law and Director of Graduate and International Legal Studies at Harvard Law School. She is a Fellow of the American Academy of Arts and Sciences and a Member of the Council on Foreign Relations. Dean Slaughter writes and lectures widely on international law and foreign policy issues. She has written over fifty articles and edited or written four books on subjects such as the effectiveness of international courts and tribunals, the legal dimensions of the war on terrorism, building global democracy, international law and international relations theory, and compliance with international rules. Her article "The Real New World Order," originally published in the 75th anniversary issue of *Foreign Affairs*, is now widely taught in colleges and universities. Her book *A New World Order* on the subject of global governance through networks of national government officials was recently published by Princeton University Press. In the summer of 2000, Dean Slaughter delivered a series of lectures on international law and international relations as part of the millennial lectures at the Hague Academy of International Law. She has been a frequent media commentator and op-ed contributor on international tribunals, terrorism, and international law. Recent publications include: "An International Constitutional Moment" (with William Burke-White), *Harvard International Law Journal* (2002); *Legalization and World Politics*, with Judith Goldstein, Miles Kahler, and Robert O. Keohane, co-editors (2001); "Building Global Democracy," *Chicago Journal of International Law* (2000); "Judicial Globalization," *Virginia Journal of International Law* (2000); "Plaintiff's Diplomacy" (with David Bosco), *Foreign Affairs* (2000); and "Governing the Global Economy Through Government Networks" in *The Role of Law in International Politics* (Michael Byers, ed., 2000). Dean Slaughter received her B.A. from Princeton University, an M. Phil. and D. Phil. from Oxford University in International Relations, and a J.D. from Harvard Law School. Before moving to Harvard Law School, she was Professor of Law and International Relations at the University of Chicago Law School from 1989 to 1994.

CARL BILDT is presently Chairman of Nordic Venture Network and Senior Adviser of IT Provider in Stockholm. With an extensive background in politics in Sweden, he is today focused on different aspects of international policy and business. In Sweden, he served as Member of Parliament from 1979 to 2001, Chairman of the Moderate Party from 1986 to 1999 and Prime Minister from 1991 to 1994. His government negotiated and signed the 1995 Swedish accession to the European Union, and undertook far-reaching liberalization and structural reforms to improve the competitiveness of Sweden and to modernize its old-style welfare system. In international affairs, he has been particularly active on the different Balkan issues. He served as European Union Special Representative to Former Yugoslavia as well as the first High Representative in Bosnia between 1995 and 1997, and then as Special Envoy of the Secretary-General of the United Nations to the Balkans between 1999 and 2001. He has also worked with space issues for the European Space Agency, and with global Internet governance issues for ICANN. Carl Bildt serves as non-executive director in a number of companies. In Sweden, these are Vostok Nafta, Lundin Petroleum, the Kreab Group as well as HiQ and Öhmans. In the United States, he serves as the only non-U.S. member of the Board of Trustees of the RAND Corporation, as non-executive Director of the global asset management company Legg Mason and Senior International Adviser to Akin Gump Strauss Hauer & Feld, a Washington-based law firm. In the field of international public policy, he serves on the Board of the Centre for European Reform as well as the Council of the International Institute for Strategic Studies in London. He is on the Editorial Board of the magazine *Russia in Global Affairs* in Moscow, and a member of the International Advisory Board of the Council on Foreign Relations in New York. He is also on the boards of Aspen Institute Italia in Rome and the Fundacion Euroamerica in Madrid. Apart from numerous other awards, he has an honorary degree from the University of St. Andrews in Scotland, where he is a Fellow at its renowned Institute for the Study of Terrorism and Political Violence.

KAZUO OGURA is President of The Japan Foundation, and a former Ambassador to Vietnam, Korea and France. A graduate of the University of Tokyo's Faculty of Law, Ambassador Ogura received his M.A. from the University of Cambridge Faculty of Economics, and his Ph.D. from Kyungwon University in 1999. After joining the Ministry of Foreign Affairs, he served in various positions, including Director-General of Economic Affairs Bureau (1992–94) and Deputy Vice-Minister for Foreign Affairs and Japanese G7/G8 Sherpa (1995–97). He is also a Visiting Researcher at the National Institute for Research Advancement and a Professor at Aoyama Gakuin University.

Table of Contents

I. Introduction

Anne-Marie Slaughter

The Westphalian order is in transition. Indeed, Carl Bildt suggests that the world may be at the outset of nothing less than a Reformation. Yet time has telescoped; we are likely to see the kinds of changes that took centuries from Martin Luther until the end of the Thirty Years War taking place across mere decades today. The pervasive sense of insecurity is real, as real as the need for new responses, new institutions, and new ideas.

Indeed, the evolution of this report itself reflects both the breadth and depth of contemporary security debates. The original question posed for this task force was the changing norms governing the legitimate use of force. That is a central question for national security experts and foreign policymakers more generally within the United States. Supporters of the Bush preemption doctrine already know how these norms should be revised; indeed, the 2002 Bush National Security Strategy could be seen as a preemptive strike on this very question. Europeans and Japanese are far more inclined to contemplate changing norms of the use of force for humanitarian protection purposes, if they countenance change at all.

But more fundamentally, each author found it very difficult to address the legitimate use of force without a wider examination of the threats we face to national and international security. That question, in turn, highlighted the extent to which the definition of security itself is up for grabs at a time of profound change in the international system. Indeed, all three essays grapple with this definition. How to integrate traditional understandings of state security—whereby the principal threat to a state's survival was posed by another state and the security of a state was largely synonymous with the security of its people—with an appreciation of the magnitude and importance of what Kazuo Ogura calls "global security issues"—terrorism, environmental degradation, international crime, infectious diseases and refugees? These issues cross borders with disdain for the divisions of national and international authority.

All three essays also accept the need for new approaches and new institutions, spending equal amounts of time on diagnosis and cure. And they recognize diverging emphases among the Trilateral countries precisely at a time when these countries need to pioneer new divisions of labor and

possibilities for collaborative action. They also highlight the growing power
of global publics to constrain as well as sanction international action.

To help organize the many ideas and proposals put forward, it may
be useful to think about five basic dichotomies. These are: state security
versus human security; hard versus soft interventions; legality versus
legitimacy; preemption versus prevention; and states versus non-state
actors. These dichotomies recur, in various guises, in each author's analysis.
They help identify important differences among the Trilateral countries
and between the Trilateral countries and the rest of the world. And they
provide a rough road-map to the obstacles and tensions that national,
regional, and global debates about security challenges and the best ways
to address them will have to address.

A key difference that emerges from these three essays merits separate
attention, particularly for the Trilateral Commission. Carl Bildt's and Kazuo
Ogura's essays reflect a security agenda that differs in important ways
from the prevailing U.S. agenda. Much of my essay reflects an awareness
of these differences and a corresponding effort to prescribe ways for the
United States to realign itself with its major allies while still recognizing
and pursuing its core interests. However, I also identify anti-Americanism
as an "ism," like communism or fascism, that is gaining its own momentum
as an ideology that radically oversimplifies a dichotomy between what
America is presumed to be and what traditional culture, religion, and
power structures are proclaimed to have been. This kind of anti-
Americanism empowers populist demagogues in many societies and
makes it increasingly difficult for governments that wish to work with
the United States to do so. It is particularly dangerous in a world in which
non-state actors can both complement and combat states.

Anti-Europeanism in the United States manifests some of the same
characteristics. It is easily exploited by opportunistic politicians, creating
an unhealthy culture of blame and externalization of domestic problems
that can in turn fuel unilateralism and possibly a return to isolationism. A
critical question for leaders of Trilateral nations will be to sort out and
address the extent to which shifting public sentiment reflects this kind of
manipulation versus what Carl Bildt refers to as the "drifting apart of the
dominating agendas" of different parts of the world.

The world faces genuine threats that are global in magnitude and will
require a coordinated global response. Different nations may, of course,
assign different priorities to those threats. But true statecraft, of the type
required to maintain and create order out of entropy, will require
developing rules and institutions that mediate genuine differences while

facilitating cooperation in the pursuit of genuine common interests. And true leadership in articulating and pursuing these common interests is likely to require the political courage necessary to stand up to popular stereotypes of nations and civilizations as well as race and religion.

State Security versus Human Security

State security is still what virtually all Americans mean when they talk about national or international security: the ability of sovereign states to defend themselves against external threats to their existence as states through conquest, military defeat, or political and economic domination. Human security is a much more recent concept, pioneered in the 1990s by the Canadian government and embraced by the UN Secretary-General and many like-minded countries. As I point out in my essay, the Commission for Human Security, launched after the UN Millennium Summit by the Government of Japan and chaired by Sadako Ogata and Amartya Sen, defines human security as the protection of "the vital core of all human lives in ways that enhance human freedoms and human fulfillment."[1] It is a definition that not only assumes that individuals rather than states are the primary actors in the international system, but that also accepts that human beings need more than protection from an invading army to lead satisfying and purposeful lives.

For Kazuo Ogura, the new challenges to national and international security are distinctive precisely because they are direct challenges to human security. He identifies a set of "global issues," which include terrorism, environmental destruction, drug trafficking, international crimes, infectious diseases, and refugee problems.[2] These are problems that affect human beings directly, even if, as is certainly the case with terrorism and quite possibly also with infectious diseases and environmental destruction, they can also threaten state security. Their solution "requires both protection and empowerment of the people. Protection implies policies, resources, and institutions to protect people, while empowerment concerns the need for the people themselves to participate in developing human resources and politico-economic support."[3]

Ogura distinguishes between three different approaches to human security, with his being the broadest. The narrowest is a focus on genocide and grave human rights violations committed by dictators or civil war

---

[1] Commission on Human Security, *Human Security Now* (New York, 2003), p. 4.
[2] Ogura essay, p. 65.
[3] Ibid., p. 65.

combatants. That is Carl Bildt's focus in much of his essay. He identifies humanitarian crises—often politically motivated—as one of the principal challenges of our age. Drawing on his experience in Kosovo, he analyzes the complex tangle of ethnic conflict, political manipulation, corruption, cruelty, and desperate human need that both draw other countries into a particular crisis and make it so hard to craft and implement an enduring solution. But at the root of these interventions are the claims of individuals to the most basic rights to life and dignity, claims that are increasingly difficult for the peoples and governments of other countries to ignore.

In my own essay I call for an integrated approach to state and human security, noting that in the United States, unlike in Europe and Japan, human security is barely on the political agenda. This relative absence is another axis of division between the United States and the rest of the world, one that reinforces the perception of the United States as fixated on military power and hence military solutions to global problems. At the same time, however, threats to state security are alive and growing. No responsible leader can ignore the possibility that a terrorist group could kill hundreds of thousands or millions of individuals with a nuclear or biological weapon, at the same time crippling a state's economic system and potentially sowing political chaos.

Hard Intervention versus Soft Intervention
Carl Bildt introduces the helpful concept of "soft interventions." The instruments of soft intervention "can range from agreements that limit the freedom of action of states in different respects to more intrusive evaluation of state policies and recommendations on how they could be changed, to even more elaborate inspections and international decisions that have to be respected."[4] A degree of soft intervention is the unavoidable flipside of growing global interdependence. By measuring types and degrees of intervention along a spectrum from hard to soft, Bildt makes clear that the foreign policy issue often in question is not *whether* to intervene or not, but *how*, a question in turn that reveals a sizable gap between the ideal and actual capacities of both individual states and international organizations in facing new international challenges.

Kazuo Ogura reminds us, however, that in many parts of the world state-building is still the order of the day, hence "[we] should not ignore the plea of many developing nations that global issues, however global their implications, should be addressed with the consent of nation-states and be based on the cooperation or collaboration among them."[5] In other

---

[4] Bildt essay, p. 43.
[5] Ogura essay, p. 66.

words, even soft interventions are still seen as incursions on national sovereignty by those countries on the receiving end. This persistent difference in perception makes the issue of legitimacy particularly important, as addressed below. It also means that we should do everything possible to avoid the need for military intervention. Soft interventions still have to be paid for, however; Ogura suggests developing a new system of burden-sharing so that "those who benefit most from the expenditure . . . bear most of the expense."[6]

I propose the development of a new generation of multilateral institutions that would be particularly valuable in carrying out many of the tasks that would qualify as soft interventions. Many of the threats to both state and human security can only be addressed by building and strengthening government capacity worldwide—the capacity of domestic governments to perform the basic governmental functions of providing order and physical security for all citizens, fair dispute resolution, a public health system, a functioning economy, and a reasonably clean environment. The best way to build and bolster this capacity is through transgovernmental networks of like government officials: police, financial regulators, health officials, environmental regulators, judges, and even legislators. These officials can offer direct material and intellectual assistance, transmit and enforce professional norms and standards, exchange valuable information, coordinate policy and collaborate on enforcement. This is a productive and valuable form of soft intervention.

Legality versus Legitimacy
The premise of all three of these essays, and indeed of the question that prompted them, is that we live in an era of old rules and new threats. The international legal rules and institutions that anchor world order were largely established after World War II, in response to the economic and political threats that had brought about two world wars and a great depression. Throughout the 1990s states used force in ways that certainly stretched the dictates of the UN Charter, culminating in the NATO intervention in Kosovo without any prior UN sanction at all. Yet a distinguished international commission appointed after the fact found that although the Kosovo intervention was illegal, it was legitimate in the eyes of the international community. The Anglo-American invasion of Iraq, on the other hand, although legally justified by the British attorney general, is almost universally regarded as illegitimate—indeed, judging by current polls, it is seen as illegal and illegitimate.

---

[6] Ibid., p. 68.

The distinction between legality and legitimacy is perhaps best understood as an artifact of transition from one legal order to another, or at least of the updating of specific legal rules to meet changing political and economic circumstances. Carl Bildt argues that any prospective "hard," e.g. military, intervention should meet the criteria of legality, legitimacy, and effectiveness, noting the complicated relationship between legality and legitimacy. He notes that an intervention that is illegal will have a harder time gaining the necessary public legitimacy. On the other hand, however, an intervention can be formally legal but still widely condemned in national, regional or global public opinion.

Both Bildt and Ogura connect the importance of legitimacy to the necessity of commanding majority support in democracies around the world. Democratically elected governments must respond to their voters as well as to the imperatives of national and international security as they define them. Indeed, Ogura closely ties the need to secure legitimacy for the use of force with the need to secure domestic and international political support. Domestically, it is the voters who must give their approval; internationally, he emphasizes the importance of non-governmental organizations, humanitarian aid agencies, and "world-wide citizens' movements."[7] These movements are often seen in stark opposition to governments, particularly developed country governments, but Ogura points out that they raise public awareness of economic, social, and ethical issues worldwide in ways that make it increasingly difficult for those governments to ignore human security issues.

Preemption versus Prevention

The Bush Administration's National Security Strategy of 2002 unilaterally declared a vastly expanded concept of the traditional international legal doctrine of preemption as a legitimate response to new security threats. The Administration's basic point, which is widely accepted as a statement of fact, although not as a predicate for preemption, is that to wait until a nuclear or biological attack by state or particularly non-state actors is "imminent" before responding is to wait too long. Doctrines developed for the days when a threat to a state's vital security interests generally meant massing armies on its borders simply won't do the job when, again, hundreds of thousands or millions of people can be killed in a single strike. Thus, for the Bush Administration, it is legitimate to preempt such threats *before* they become imminent.

---

[7] Ibid., p. 70-71.

The better view, at least based on these three essays, is that preemption should give way to prevention. A preemptive strike once a threat has emerged, whether it is "imminent" or near-imminent, or potentially imminent, is a poor and likely ineffective substitute for a policy of preventing its emergence in the first place. Bildt reminds us that according to the European Security Strategy, "conflict prevention and threat prevention cannot start too early."[8] Ogura warns that prevention is the only way to address some of the most important threats to human security, such as disease and environmental degradation. And I argue, building on previous work done with Lee Feinstein, that UN members should acknowledge a duty to prevent states without internal checks on their power from acquiring or using weapons of mass destruction.[9]

For all three authors, an emphasis on prevention over preemption also means a privileging of non-military responses to threats over military ones as much as possible, including much more emphasis on the development of incentive-based rather than sanction-based approaches to dealing with nations such as North Korea several years ago or Iran today. Many of these approaches would fall into the category of soft interventions. Virtually all would require much more burden-sharing among Trilateral countries and others.

State versus Non-State Actors
The central premise of Carl Bildt's essay is that we are entering a post-Westphalian era, in which "the two main pillars of the Westphalian order," absolute state sovereignty over domestic affairs and the preeminence of states as actors in the international system, are "starting to crumble."[10] Among the principal challenges to this order is the ability of "small bands of dedicated individuals . . . to threaten the fundamental interests of the most powerful of states."[11] Insurgents within states, often bringing about state failure or even implosion, often pose as powerful threats to the region or even the world as the governments they are challenging.

Terrorists are non-state actors, but so too are environmentalists, human rights activists, and aid workers—prime protagonists in global civil society. Indeed, Kazuo Ogura argues that NGOs increasingly fill the gap between the roles of nation states and international organizations and that

---

[8] Bildt essay, p. 54
[9] Lee Feinstein and Anne-Marie Slaughter, "A Duty to Prevent," *Foreign Affairs*, vol. 83, no. 1, January/February 2004, pp. 136-151.
[10] Bildt essay, p. 37.
[11] Ibid., p. 37.

"we have to rely more . . . [on them], particularly in the area of human security."[12] He worries that one of the consequences is the erosion of norms of neutrality for international humanitarian workers, as they come to be identified with international organizations or even with states that are actively taking sides in a conflict. Can their special and protected role as non-state actors in a world of states protect them against other non-state actors? And if they come to need protection, it is likely to come from state forces, which will make their neutrality ever more suspect.

Another way to think about state versus non-state actors is to differentiate between governments, the sole representatives of their states in the traditional Westphalian order, and their citizens, who increasingly have direct influence in international affairs as the holders of individual human rights and as collective publics that can sharply constrain their governments' actions. This is certainly not the conventional definition of non-state actors, but it is yet another way that actors other than states help to define the post-Westphalian order. This is the context in which I argue that anti-Americanism poses a threat not only to the U.S. government, but to all governments that would side with it in meeting global challenges.

Conclusion

Perhaps the most striking feature of these three essays is that while they set out to identify new threats to international security, they all agree on a redefinition of international sovereignty. They either directly or indirectly endorse the conception of sovereignty put forth by the International Commission on Intervention and State Sovereignty, chaired by Gareth Evans and Evans Sahnoun, in a report entitled *The Responsibility to Protect*.[13] The central idea in this report is that UN membership, as entailed by accepting the obligations of the Charter, requires a state to protect its own citizens from death or serious human rights violations. Failure to fulfill this responsibility entitles other states to intervene under UN auspices.

Sovereignty as responsibility rather than autonomy—or, alternatively, as a conditioned autonomy—recognizes the reality of deep interdependence, of a global condition in which a government genuinely

---

[12] Ogura essay, p. 67-68
[13] International Commission on Intervention and State Sovereignty, *The Responsibility to Protect*, (Ottawa, Canada: International Development Research Center, 2004).

cannot perform its most essential functions of guaranteeing order, health, and a functioning economy without paying attention to what happens in other states. It also recognizes that the first obligation to provide human security rests with national governments rather than international institutions. However, if a national government fails to safeguard its citizens from death and disaster, the international community can and should identify the resultant threat to human security within a nation as a threat to international security.

Sovereignty as responsibility is an important part of a new calculus of international order. It is not enough, however. The exercise of identifying new threats to national and international security, throughout the Trilateral countries and beyond, is the first step in a longer and more complex process of assessing how well national and international institutions are equipped to meet those threats. Those institutions, in turn, uphold and implement fundamental norms of both stability and justice, the foundations of an ordered world.

As the analysis in these three essays suggests, we need both new rules and tools. And we need to formulate both our problems and proposed solutions together—both within the Trilateral countries and with many others. On each of the dichotomies outlined above, Americans diverge noticeably from both Europeans and many Asians. The American debates on national security focus more on state security than human security, more on hard intervention than soft intervention, more on legitimacy than legality, more on preemption than prevention, and more on state than non-state actors. In a world of rising and vehement anti-Americanism, those divergences are of particular concern and should be a particular focus of the Trilateral dialogue. May it play a vital role in making common cause to face common threats.

II. A North American Perspective

Old Rules, New Threats:
Terrorism, Proliferation, and Anti-Americanism

Anne-Marie Slaughter

Executive Summary

The principal threats to international security are 1) the prospective intersection of terrorism and technology, allowing a terrorist group to acquire and/or use either nuclear or biological weapons capable of killing millions of people; 2) the proliferation of nuclear, biological, and, to a lesser extent, chemical weapons to states hostile to the United States and/or to other states in their region; and 3) the rise of global anti-Americanism, which poses a threat not only to the United States but creates a new axis of enmity in the world that destabilizes domestic politics, roils alliances, and undermines our collective ability to focus productively and constructively on threats to global health, the environment, and the development of all the world's people. These are threats to state security as traditionally defined, but they also affect our collective ability to respond to threats to human security worldwide.

We must meet these threats both conceptually and practically. Conceptually, we must redefine our understanding of international security to include both state and human security. This is the only way to forge a consensus among all the world's nations, developed and developing, regarding the nature of the threats we face and the best strategies to respond. An integrated conception of state and human security in turn requires a deeper shift in the definition of sovereignty itself, from sovereignty as autonomy to sovereignty as collective responsibility and capacity to participate in international institutions.

Practically, we must reform existing multilateral institutions and create a generation of new global institutions that are better designed to mobilize as many government officials as possible who have authority to address specific problems in as many states as possible and to build their capacity to do so. Within existing institutions, beginning with the United Nations, connecting state security and human security means linking the human rights side of the UN with the Security Council by treating indicators of how a government treats its own people as relevant to the threat it poses to other nations. A new generation of institutions should be network-based, designed to expand and strengthen informal networks of justice ministers, financial regulators of all kinds, customs and immigration officials, intelligence operatives, environmental regulators, judges, and legislators in ways that will allow us to build and draw on a global governance capacity operating on the ground in countries around the world. These networks will benefit from the information revolution; together with civil society and corporate networks they can also be valuable conduits for accurate information aimed at all the world's peoples.

The United States should lead the way in calling for and creating this new generation of global institutions, working closely with the EU and other like-minded nations. By showing imagination and enterprise in helping to equip the world to face threats to both nation-states and their people, the United States can reduce the percentage in manipulating anti-Americanism for personal or ideological gain. It will thereby enhance both U.S. and global security.

Introduction

We live in an era of self-conscious historical change, in which an old order appears to be giving way to a new one. Non-state groups are making war and threatening states; weapons of mass destruction are proliferating; the internal affairs of some states increasingly affect the external security of others; and global threats such as HIV/AIDS and climate change cannot be tackled successfully even by the world's most powerful nations. The collective security system established in 1945 through the United Nations and subsequently through a variety of regional organizations was designed to address a very different set of threats. The challenge today is to adapt those institutions and perhaps to create new ones to address the threats of a changing world.

To meet this challenge, it is first necessary to agree on the nature of the principal threats that must be countered. And here's the rub. As is evident even from the three essays presented in this volume, the discussion of threats in the United States, Europe, and Japan proceeds quite differently. Most striking is the differential emphasis on state security versus human security—a term that is barely heard in Washington but appears to dominate in Tokyo and receives considerable attention in Berlin, Paris, and Brussels. Moving further south, or indeed simply to the corridors of the UN, the conversation quickly turns to the threats posed by civil and ethnic conflict, private violence fueled by the small arms trade, disease, and grinding poverty. These are the threats killing tens of millions each year.

This essay begins (Part A) by identifying the principal new challenges to international security as seen from the U.S. perspective. Part B turns to the conceptual challenge of developing an integrated concept of state and human security that will prove workable as the basis for a grand political bargain between developed and developing countries and indeed among the United States, Europe, and Japan. Part C proposes a set of reforms for existing international institutions, principally the United Nations, that would build on this integrated concept of security to spell out clear international obligations applicable to all states combined with the ability to single out states that pose a particular threat to their own citizens or their fellow states and take collective action in response.

Part D proposes a new set of multilateral institutions built around networks of national government officials. These institutions have the potential to be more inclusive, more flexible, and more effective in addressing contemporary global problems, particularly when they are combined with existing international institutions in various ways. For instance, just as the G-20 group of finance ministers from a representative group of countries around the world now plays an important role in governing the global economy, a G-20 of leaders, perhaps with a varying membership depending on the issue at hand, could be constituted to operate within the United Nations and/or as a bridge between the United Nations and the Bretton Woods institutions. Part E closes with more specific policy recommendations.

A. The Challenges

National security debates in the United States are obsessed with the use of force. Consider the following claim from former Under Secretary of Defense for Policy Walter Slocombe: "No question has more preoccupied discussions of international law and international relations than that of the legitimacy and wisdom of the use of force."[1] The most frequent answer to this question is a turn to prevention rather than preemption, and certainly rather than reaction. These debates focus almost exclusively on state security. The only mention of issues that much of the rest of the world

---

[1] Walter B. Slocombe, "Force, Pre-emption and Legitimacy," *Survival*, vol. 45, no. 1, Spring 2003, pp. 117-130.

worries about under the rubric of human security—chaos, anarchy, civil violence—comes under the heading of failed states as a breeding ground for terrorism that can in turn threaten state security.

1. Looking through the U.S. Lens: Principal Threats to State Security

The principal threats to international security, from the U.S. or perhaps the Anglo-American perspective, are:

- **The intersection of terrorism and weapons of mass destruction (WMD).** The most immediate and most dangerous threat to U.S. national security is the potential destruction of an American city or cities by means of a terrorist act using a nuclear weapon. Closely related is the threat of the release of biological agents in any forum (the subway) where many people could be infected and then spread the disease; or the similar use of chemical weapons. This threat leads to two principal corollaries:
  o The threat of failed or failing states that could become ideal sites for terrorist groups to train cadres and plan operations.
  o Proliferation of WMD to states that do or could support terrorists.

- **Proliferation of WMD to states hostile to the United States.** North Korea and Iran pose a threat to the United States independent of their actual or potential support for terrorists; Libya and Iraq after Saddam Hussein are barely emerging from this category. If these governments gain nuclear weapons in particular, they would be in a position to exercise nuclear blackmail on specific issues, or at least to threaten it; to destabilize their regions either by triggering an arms race or by threatening neighboring countries; and to pass on WMD technology to client states.

- **Global anti-Americanism.** Rising anti-American sentiment worldwide, particularly among but by no means limited to Islamic countries, poses a long-term threat to U.S. national security interests by making it increasingly difficult even for friendly governments to cooperate with the U.S. government in pursuit of U.S. objectives. Conversely, leaders can increasingly get elected on aggressively anti-American platforms. The centrality of anti-Americanism in domestic political debates in countries around the world creates a new axis of enmity, allowing extremist leaders to exploit anti-American sentiment for a host of purposes and rallying many of the world's frustrated and dispossessed around the illusion of a common cause.

The first two of these threats need little elaboration. They are the top of the U.S. list of security threats and are by no means limited to the United States. Use of a weapon of mass destruction—particularly a nuclear or a biological weapon—in a major city in the United States or aimed primarily at U.S. citizens abroad would unavoidably kill the nationals from many nations—as the September 11th attacks did. Equally important, use of a nuclear weapon would break "the nuclear taboo," which has had its own impact on restraining nations from using the weapons they possess. Similarly, a large-scale biological attack would catapult the entire world into a new era of bioweapons and biosecurity—an era often predicted but as yet prevented from full realization.

The third threat, anti-Americanism, would not appear on many standard lists of threats, and to the extent it does is likely to be regarded as further evidence of the kind of American ethnocentrism that helps fuel anti-Americanism in the first place. But my point is not that what threatens America automatically threatens the world. Nor is it simply that anti-Americanism makes it harder for the U.S. government to get things done when it seeks cooperation. On the contrary, anti-Europeanism is rising in many parts of the United States in ways that should be equally worrying European leaders who count on the reality and the potential of transatlantic cooperation on a host of issues. In both cases, the larger danger is the intersection between an over-simplified "anti-X" and the volatility and instability of mass democratic politics.

Anti-Americanism thus becomes a national and global security threat to the extent that it is creating a dangerous domestic political dynamic in countries around the world: an invitation to demagoguery. As an "ism," rather than opposition to specific U.S. policies, anti-Americanism is developing its own momentum, becoming an easy and simplistic axis of division for any politician to exploit. Those seeking to stay in power can manipulate it to deflect what would otherwise be internal opposition. Those seeking to gain power have a ready-made "them" against which to build, in time-honored fascist, communist, and now fundamentalist fashion, an "us." The result is that anti-Americanism is not just a problem for Americans and, at the same time, that it is a far bigger problem for Americans than one election can easily fix.

The other point worthy of note regarding this list of three principal threats is what is not there. Other headings in the Bush Administration's National Security Strategy promulgated in September 2002 include the promotion of human dignity, free trade and free markets, democratization, and "cooperative action with the other main centers of global power."[2] President Bush has sharply increased the proportion of the U.S. budget allocated to foreign aid; he has also promised $15 billion to fight HIV/ AIDS as a global scourge. Nevertheless, the dark threat seen stalking both America and the world in Washington circles is compounded principally of terrorism, radicalism, and technology. The equally potent mixture of disease, poverty, illiteracy, ethnic conflict, and private violence that much of the rest of the world defines as a threat to "human security" rather than "state security" receives little more than lip-service.

2. Are Threats to Human Security Really "Threats"?

The division between the proponents of state security versus human security is more than just a disagreement about whether the security of states or the security of individuals is more important. The deeper rift involves the utility or even the relevance of inter-state force to the threats that render millions and indeed billions of the world's people insecure— public and private violence resulting from internal conflict, small arms proliferation, poverty, and disease. The Commission for Human Security, launched after the UN Millennium Summit by the Government of Japan and chaired by Sadako Ogata and Amartya Sen, has observed: "The state remains the fundamental purveyor of security. Yet it often fails to fulfill its security obligations—and at times has even become a source of threat to its own people."[3] Human security aims to "protect the vital core of all human lives in ways that enhance human freedoms and human fulfillment."[4] These goals suggest what is traditionally a development agenda far more than a security agenda.

Further, the traditional national security community in the United States and indeed in Britain and France is actively hostile to the idea of expanding the notion of "threats to security" to include concerns about disease, poverty, illiteracy, and private violence. Except for private violence, it is argued, these are not "threats" at all, but rather long-standing social ills that cannot be combated through the apparatus of national and international security structures. Further, they so dilute the meaning of "threat" that it becomes impossible to focus on the "real threats" of terrorism, WMD, failed states, ethnic conflict, etc. The standard rejoinder,

---

[2] White House, *The National Security Strategy of the United States of America* (Washington, D.C.: U.S. Government Printing Office, September 2002).
[3] Commission on Human Security, *Human Security Now* (New York, 2003), p. 2.
[4] Ibid., p. 4.

of course, is that issues such as poverty and disease are not "threats" only for those who have never faced them.

In fact, however, state security and human security are closely intertwined—the collapse of a state can plunge its population into even greater poverty and violence; conversely, improving the health of a population often requires strengthening state apparatus that can in turn strengthen basic civil order and improve the ability to detect and eliminate terrorist cells, as well as to divert state resources from a particular government's pursuit of weapons of mass destruction to the broader welfare of its people. But which strategy to pursue first? And what happens when short-term and long-term strategies conflict? What is the best combined approach to assuring both state and human security? These are the issues that are most likely to divide the developed from the developing world, and possibly the developed world itself.

B. Redefining Security and Sovereignty

How do we think about state security and human security simultaneously and develop an integrated approach to attaining both? The time for developing such an approach is ripe. Recent revelations about the difficulties U.S. policymakers had in grasping the extent of the threat posed by al Qaeda before September 11th reflects in part the grip of a Cold War mentality that focuses only on states as the principal actors in the international system. Similarly, efforts to develop a new or revised collective security system through the UN must involve some kind of "grand bargain" between the developed and the developing world regarding a combined effort to address threats to both state and human security. At the same time, however, fashionable notions in the 1990s about "the end of the state" or the withering away of state power are evidently wide of the mark. Without state power and resources, and without strengthening the power and resources of fledgling and failing states in many parts of the world, we cannot hope to help individuals, in terms of human security, or counter them, in terms of state security.

1. Security as Protection from Violent Death, Injury, or Subjugation
In its simplest form, security means protection from violence. That is the most basic service that any government must provide its citizens; indeed, it is the complete breakdown of law and order, typically signaled by widespread violence from marauding gangs or insurgents of various kinds, that leads to the diagnosis of a failed state. The traditional difference between domestic and international security has been a matter of scale,

which in turn has been assumed to be an indicator of the source of the threat—individuals versus states. A pattern of individual deaths, even if systematic, was deemed to be the result of organized crime; mass violence indicated backing by a rival state. Indeed, the apparent certainty of some policymakers in the United States and other countries that attacks like September 11th must have been backed or even sponsored by a state rather than a network of individual terrorists reflects precisely this mindset.[5]

Well before September 11th, however, Thomas Friedman wrote about the "super-empowered individual," who could pose threats to international security of a kind previously the province only of states.[6] At the same time, persistent threats to individual security within a state, previously the province only of domestic governments, merit international engagement. Part of the point of the human security movement is that omnipresent fear of the loss of life through violence feels the same whether the imagined enemy is a soldier, a terrorist, a warlord, or a gang-leader. If governments fail to fulfill their most basic function, then the responsibility devolves to the international community. A revised definition of "international security" would thus drop the distinction between domestic and international as such and speak instead of "global security": an effort at every level—local, national, regional, and global—to protect individuals from violence.

This integrated conception of security is easiest to grasp when we see the integrated nature of the response to the threats that menace both individuals and states. A large part of the strategy to address all three of the threats identified above must be to promote, build, and insist on decent and effective governments worldwide through every means possible. Part of that strategy will require restoring or building state governing capacity at the domestic level—providing a wide range of resources, training, and ongoing advice and support to enable governments to control the individuals who have disrupted social order within a particular state. This is precisely the same capacity that is necessary to identify and root out terrorist cells within a particular nation, as well as to participate in blocking such sources of support as financing and arms supply. It is also the capacity necessary to ensure that states can fulfill their international treaty obligations, and, critically, to ensure that other states and non-state actors

---

[5] See, e.g. Richard A. Clarke, *Against All Enemies: Inside America's War on Terror* (New York: Free Press, 2004), p. 30.
[6] Thomas L. Friedman, *The Lexus and the Olive Tree* (New York: Farrar, Straus, Giroux, 1999).

can monitor them in the process.[7] At the same time, of course, rebuilding and strengthening governing capacity is an important part of the solution for addressing non-violent threats to human welfare such as persistent poverty, illiteracy, and disease.

Individuals are part of the solution as well as part of the problem. Sadako Ogata writes, for instance, that "The [Human Security] Commission focuses on people as the main stake holders of ensuring security. By people, we refer particularly to communities that bind individuals along ethnic, religious, social links and values. Public opinion and civil society organizations play an increasingly important role in the prevention of violent conflicts as well as the eradication of poverty."[8] Mobilizing the non-profit and the private sectors in countries around the world to work in partnership with domestic governments in ways that can strengthen governing capacity is likely to be more effective than working with governments alone. Indeed, some corporations are beginning to assume responsibility for controlling civil violence and even for conflict resolution in parts of the world that they work in.[9] Further, focusing on domestic governance capacity and engaging individuals within states help to shift the normal developed-developing world dynamic away from always seeking to constrain developing country behavior toward actually creating more opportunity for developing country citizens.

2. Sovereignty as Responsibility

At the deepest level, meeting the security challenges of a new century will require changing our understanding and implementation of sovereignty itself. Such a proposition would normally be a subject more for academic journals than a Trilateral Commission report, except that the UN Secretary General himself has already put it on the table. Perhaps more surprising still, the International Commission for Intervention and State Sovereignty (ICISS) took on precisely the redefinition of sovereignty, arguing that the core meaning of UN membership must change from "the final symbol of independent sovereign statehood and thus the seal of acceptance into the

---

[7] See generally Abram Chayes and Antonia Handler Chayes, *The New Sovereignty: Compliance with International Regulatory Agreements* (Cambridge, MA: Harvard University Press, 1995).

[8] Sadako Ogata, "Empowering People for Human Security," Payne Lecture, Stanford University, May 28, 2003.

[9] Virginia Haufer, "Partnering with the Private Sector for Conflict Management," Paper prepared for the Annual Meeting of the International Studies Association, New Orleans, March 24-27, 2002.

community of nations," to recognition of a state "as a responsible member of the community of nations."[10]

On this view, nations are free to choose whether or not to sign the Charter. If they do, however, they must accept the "responsibilities of membership" flowing from their signature. According to the ICISS, "There is no transfer or dilution of state sovereignty. But there is a necessary re-characterization involved: from *sovereignty as control* to *sovereignty as responsibility* in both internal functions and external duties" (emphasis in the original).[11] Internally, a government has a responsibility to respect the dignity and basic rights of its citizens; externally, it has a responsibility to respect the sovereignty of other states.

Interestingly, this language and the underlying concepts are not far from George Shultz's insistence that we must work "with aspirations for a world of states that recognize accountability for human freedom and dignity."[12] The Bush National Security Strategy similarly begins with a focus on the promotion of human dignity, which requires liberty, as the underlying aim of all American national security policy. The underlying paradigm shift, as the ICISS recognizes, is to understand sovereignty as conferring responsibilities as well as rights: responsibilities that flow initially to a government's own people and secondarily to its fellow states.

Redefining sovereignty as responsibility is conceptually sound and rhetorically appealing, but ultimately meaningless unless it can be operationalized. Translating this conception of sovereignty into practice requires two critical corollaries:

1) **The international community has a collective responsibility to provide whatever assistance is necessary and effective to enable individual governments to meet their responsibilities to their citizens.**

2) **Failure to meet these responsibilities on the part of an individual government can be the basis for collective sanction and differential treatment by the international community.**

The first of these corollaries is positive and likely to be far more politically palatable. It speaks to the legitimate insistence on the part of

---

[10] International Commission on Intervention and State Sovereignty, *The Responsibility to Protect*, (Ottawa, Canada: International Development Research Center, 2004), p. 13.
[11] Ibid.
[12] George P. Shultz, "A Changed World," Third Annual Kissinger Lecture at the Library of Congress, Feb. 11, 2004

developing countries that the international community pay greater attention to the plight of their citizens, while at the same time conditioning an obligation of international assistance on demonstrated effectiveness. The second corollary will be more controversial, yet flows equally from the logic of the responsibility to protect.

Rethinking sovereignty and adopting collective duties to ensure that all states live up to individual and collective responsibilities are far-reaching propositions. But as Carl Bildt argues forcefully, we no longer live in a Westphalian world, in which sovereignty means above all the right to be left alone. On the contrary, in the words of the Human Security Commission, we are "living in a world more interdependent than ever before. All societies depend much more on the acts or omissions of others for the security of their people, even for their survival."[13] In the Westphalian system, a state's sovereignty has always been conditional on its meeting its obligations to its fellow states, in the sense that a breach of those obligations, such as threatening or breaching the peace or committing an act of aggression, would trigger collective sanctions. An interdependent conception of sovereignty means that a state is equally subject to sanction for violating its obligations to its own citizens, obligations equally established by international law.

C. Reforming Existing Institutions

The next step toward operationalizing a revised conception of security and sovereignty is to reform existing international institutions—beginning with the United Nations—to implement the twin corollaries of collective assistance and collective sanction to enable governments to meet their obligations to their own citizens and to sanction them if they do not. The blueprint for such reform is once again conceptually simple but politically difficult. An enormous and important amount of UN machinery is devoted to propagating and enforcing human rights law, holding governments to account for torturing, murdering, disappearing, and otherwise oppressing their own people. Another part is devoted to trying to regulate the use of armed force. Yet the two halves are rarely if ever joined.

Conceptually, again, the origins of the Universal Declaration of Human Rights reflect in part the recognition that Hitler's horrific abuses of his own people foreshadowed the threat he posed to the world. The International Commission on Intervention and State Sovereignty's recommendations concerning intervention for the purposes of

---

[13] *Human Security Now*, p. 12.

humanitarian protection built in part on that ongoing recognition. The ICISS recommends that if a state has failed to live up to its responsibility to protect its citizens under a number of detailed and carefully delineated circumstances, then its fellow states have the right to intervene for equally carefully specified objectives. For a state to be subject to intervention for purposes of humanitarian protection, it must have demonstrably harmed its citizens itself or be manifestly unable to rescue them from harm done by others.

Similarly, Feinstein and Slaughter have called for a collective "duty to prevent," whereby all members of the United Nations, preferably acting through the Security Council, have a duty to prevent states without internal checks on their power from acquiring or using weapons of mass destruction.[14] In the humanitarian protection category, the government in question has either failed or is itself a menace to its people. In the non-proliferation category, the greatest danger is that a state can acquire, develop, deploy, or transfer nuclear or biological weapons capable of killing millions of people with one strike before other governments have had a chance to respond. The most important commodity in fighting this threat is information. Governments without internal checks on their power have no independent media, no opposition parties, and typically no means even for political dissidents to challenge the government or communicate to others outside the country. In such conditions, given any evidence that such a government is trying to attain WMD, its fellow governments must assume the worst for their own protection and act quickly and collectively to compel the production of evidence and to ensure that the government in question complies with its existing international legal obligations.

The tricky question here is how to determine when a government falls into this category. *Ad hoc* determinations, even on the part of the Security Council, are too vulnerable to abuse based on political motivation. Further, many governments have *some* checks on their power, but relatively weak and partial ones. What is needed is revision of the Non-Proliferation Treaty to create a tripwire of some kind focused on a willingness to provide maximum information about nuclear activities to the International Atomic Energy Association (IAEA) in the context of suspected illegality. If a state refuses to provide such information, the Security Council could be mobilized quickly to focus global attention on the problem and develop a list of preventive measures that then could be implemented on a fairly rapid basis.

---

[14] Lee Feinstein and Anne-Marie Slaughter, "A Duty to Prevent," *Foreign Affairs*, vol. 83, no. 1, January/February 2004, pp. 136-151.

Any such reform of the United Nations decision-making mechanisms is most likely to take place practically in terms of a revised set of understandings of the meaning of a "threat to the peace" in the language of article 39, as well as building a greater capacity to act with inducements and support to nations posing such a threat as well as with coercive measure. Such reform will also require a host of safeguards and caveats. To begin with, the great powers of the world, most notably the United States, will have to recommit to genuine multilateral constraints on the decision to use force in anything but a defensive mode. This does not mean, as the current Administration would have it, that the United States has to "get permission" to defend its vital interests. Its decision to go to war in Afghanistan was generally viewed as a legitimate exercise of its right of self-defense under article 51. But it means that a decision to use force in any case other than the traditional view of preemption, when an attack is demonstrably imminent, must be taken collectively, ideally through the Security Council or some other UN mechanism.

Second, the principal members of the UN, meaning the P-5 plus, must take special efforts to spell out guiding principles and conditions that will attach to any collective decision to intervene, forcibly or nonforcibly, in areas that have traditionally fallen within the "domestic jurisdiction" of member states. Many participants in U.S. national security debates fail to understand the extent to which concerns about the selective abuse of any power to intervene dominates debates in the rest of the world, including Europe. The "West versus the rest" has increasingly given way in many quarters to "the U.S. versus the rest," meaning that *any* legitimation of the use of force, or even more broadly, any loosening of the foundational norm of non-intervention, is seen as subject to selective application by the United States either within the Security Council or on its own. The U.S. obsession with the threat posed by Iraq while downplaying concerns about North Korea; the emphasis on the "axis of evil"; and the U.S. willingness to turn a relatively blind eye to the development and dissemination of nuclear weapons by Pakistan as long as the Pakistani government cooperates in a U.S. search for Osama Bin Laden have all fueled these fears.

Further, many Europeans, and indeed many members of the U.S. human rights community, worry that the best may be the enemy of the good: that any effort to broaden norms regarding the use of force to address concerns about the intersection of terrorism and WMD will undo the slow progress made in the 1990s toward a carefully conscribed norm of intervention for the purposes of humanitarian protection. The "responsibility to protect" was bold enough, and only gained consensus within the ICISS due to the intensive and laborious process of spelling out every detail of when and how such a responsibility could be triggered at the collective level. Similar caution and precision must be exercised in defining precisely how evidence of grave and systematic human rights abuses within countries can be used as evidence of a security threat justifying and indeed requiring collective action by the Security Council.

D. Creating a new Generation of Multilateral Institutions

No amount of reform of existing institutions can ultimately meet the new threats we face. These threats, and the integrated response to them proposed here, require a new generation of multilateral institutions. These institutions must draw on and mobilize all parts of our governments. They must be based on the premise that states remain the primary and indispensable actors in the international system but they have become multi-dimensional actors. They are no longer represented chiefly by their head of state, foreign minister, or delegated ambassadors. Rather, they increasingly operate in the international system in the way they operate domestically—as a collection of individuals who operate through defined institutions such as courts, legislatures, ministries, and regulatory agencies. These individuals are networking with their foreign counterparts, creating transgovernmental networks dedicated to effective global financial regulation, criminal law enforcement, more efficient dispute resolution, intelligence sharing, etc.[15]

These networks, in turn, are already playing an important role in the U.S.-led "war" on terrorism—enabling critical cooperation among justice ministers, intelligence agencies, financial regulators, police, prosecutors, and investigators across borders on the trail of terrorist networks. Whereas military responses to terrorism, as in Afghanistan or Iraq, are typically the province of the "unitary" state, these networks reflect and extend the capacity of the state acting through its component institutions.[16] The current regulation of the global economy operates as much through these "government networks" as it does through traditional inter-governmental institutions.

Yet we have only begun to tap the full capacity of these networks, particularly in two critical areas for meeting challenges to international security: 1) bolstering human security in states around the world, and 2) providing post-conflict state-building services. In both categories, networks

---

[15] See Anne-Marie Slaughter, *A New World Order* (Princeton: Princeton University Press, 2004).

[16] I have elsewhere termed this the "disaggregated state."

of national government officials in areas from utilities regulation to criminal justice, and including legislators and judges, can serve as transmission belts for knowledge, training, material assistance and human support for their counterparts in developing countries generally as well as in post-conflict states and transitional democracies. Indeed, many of these networks already provide such assistance, in areas such as securities and environmental regulation, as well as judicial training. But far more could be done.

In helping to strengthen domestic governance capacity and thereby help meet human security needs, government networks are at the same time strengthening our collective capacity to meet threats to state security such as terrorism and WMD proliferation. They also ensure that the responsibility for meeting national and international security threats devolves beyond the foreign and defense ministries in all states, requiring a much larger proportion of domestic officials to engage with their foreign counterparts and to learn from them as well as teach. Just as terrorists can penetrate our society, defenses must penetrate our government.

A coordinated global response to a new generation of security threats would thus emphasize not only the reform of existing international institutions, but also the creation, or in many cases the formalization, of new ones. To take a concrete example, the G-20 is currently an informal group of finance ministers from many of the same countries that would be eligible for membership on a reformed Security Council. Creation of a G-20 at leaders' level would include most of the current G-20 members (the G-8 plus Australia, Argentina, Brazil, China, India, Indonesia, Mexico, Saudi Arabia, South Africa, South Korea, Turkey, and the EU) with perhaps a variable additional membership depending on the issue involved. An "L-20" could then operate within the United Nations or as a bridge between the United Nations and the Bretton Woods institutions.

These leaders would have the ability to convene and task networks of their ministers and judges in virtually any area of human and state security, networks that would in turn work within or at least with other existing international institutions. Those networks could be expanded to be made as representative as possible of different groups of countries. They could be given greater resources to use in helping their members build capacity. And they could be given defined decision-making power in limited areas, subject to oversight by networks of both state actors—most likely legislators—and NGOs.

The United States should take the lead in creating this new generation of institutions, working closely with the EU and other like-minded nations. Current anti-Americanism is fueled by forces deeper than dislike of any

one U.S. administration or any specific set of policies. Indeed, it is often
fanned by governments that are official U.S. allies. But the U.S. government
can do much to reduce the political profit in anti-Americanism. Above all,
it can begin by once again leading *with* other nations rather than against
them. Institutionalizing cooperation in the service of common goals,
through institutions which constrain as well as enable all their members,
is the right place to start.

E. Matching Threats and Responses

The world faces a set of threats and a distribution of capabilities that call
for more than incremental responses. Leaders who would seize the
initiative to shape and define the historical transition we can sense but
barely grasp must respond with bold ideas and the determination and
collaboration necessary to see them implemented. How then do the
proposals advanced above respond to the three threats listed at the outset
of this essay: 1) the intersection of terrorism and weapons of mass
destruction; 2) the proliferation of weapons of mass destruction to states
hostile to the United States; and 3) global anti-Americanism? (As noted
above, this listing reflects an assessment of global security threats from a
primarily U.S. perspective, but it is by no means limited to the United
States.) And how can these proposals be actually implemented?

To begin with, the rise of terrorism as a threat reflects a world
sufficiently globalized and technologically advanced that although states
remain the primary players in the international system, individuals can
also increasingly rally public support and build an infrastructure of
aggression that was once available only to states. Thus any concept of
security must address the wellsprings of individual anger and despair.
This is not to endorse simplistic equations like "poverty breeds terrorism."
But it is to acknowledge the increased complexity of security calculations,
in which threats to individuals can mutate and evolve into threats to states.
A sea-change of this magnitude requires a profound conceptual shift to
create a new foundation for a host of smaller proposals. To that end,

1)   **The United Nations Eminent Persons Panel should
     develop an integrated concept of human and state
     security as the basis for an updated understanding of
     the obligations imposed by the UN Charter.**

Second, the threat of proliferation of WMD, particularly nuclear
weapons, to states deeply and even irrationally hostile to the United States
—and indeed to their neighbors—exposes additional profound flaws in
the existing institutional framework for addressing international security

threats. The rules governing the use of force embedded in the UN Charter are reactive rather than proactive. They are designed for a world of armies massing on borders rather than to protect against the development of weapons that can obliterate millions in an instant. We need to adapt these rules to meet these threats and to allow the Security Council and other parts of the UN to act early enough to prevent proliferation to governments that have little or no internal checks on their power. Such prevention should begin far upstream of any contemplated use of force, but neither can the force be a weapon only of last resort.

2) **The Security Council should adopt an updated set of principles regarding the proper interpretation of "a breach of the peace, threat to the peace, or act of aggression" in article 39 of the UN Charter. These principles must include guidelines for preventive action, both non-coercive and coercive, in cases involving governments with little or no internal checks on their power and hence the ability to abuse that power on a catastrophic scale. At the same time, the Security Council, working together with the IAEA, should develop a series of proxy measures designed to distinguish governments acting in good faith to comply with their legal obligations from those that are not.**

Third, we must shift the dominant power dynamic in the world from one in which the United States proclaims its leadership and challenges all nations to "be with us or against us," triggering either reluctant cooperation by governments without their publics or fierce rejection, to one of institutionalized cooperation on the part of all like-minded nations to fight common threats including terrorism, AIDS and other global epidemics, and global warming. Led by the United States, nations should institutionalize and expand many existing networks of government officials engaged in financial regulation, domestic law and order, border control, environmental protection, intelligence gathering, and other areas as ways of tackling global challenges by both promulgating rules and practices and building the capacity to implement them in as many countries as possible.

3) **A new U.S. administration should work with Canadian Prime Minister Paul Martin to convene a version of the existing G-20 of Finance Ministers as a leaders group to help try to break international logjams over issues such as agricultural subsidies in the developed world, either directly or again through their ability to convene**

networks of the relevant ministers, such as trade, agriculture, and development ministers. The United States should then join with the EU to create a Global Justice Network (of Justice Ministers); a Global Transparency Network (of top officials working to counter money laundering and other financial crimes, bringing together existing smaller networks); a Global Health Network (of Health Ministers); and similar networks as needed.

Conclusion

The world faces a new set of threats, in which individuals can do damage on a scale once reserved to states and states can often no longer protect their citizens from organized and systematic violence. State security and human security are deeply intertwined and must be addressed through integrated national and global strategies. The process of redefining security leads in turn to a revised conception of sovereignty, from a right to be left alone to a responsibility to protect individual citizens and the right and capacity to participate with other nations in upholding and enforcing that responsibility. Existing international institutions must be reformed to connect the parts addressing human security with the parts addressing state security. And a new generation of institutions must be created, based on networks of nation officials, to harness and steer the capacities of all government officials in as many governments as possible to help one another establish stable and effective national and global governance. In all of this, the United States must join forces with the EU and other important countries around the world, finding a way to lead that does not generate its own liabilities, fueling anti-Americanism as a destructive political force of its own

III. A European Perspective

Peace and War in the World after Westphalia: Some Reflections on the Challenges of a Changing International Order

Carl Bildt

It belongs to the conventional wisdom to date the emergence of the present international order to the great settlements after the Thirty Years War in Europe. The Peace of Westphalia in 1648 is normally seen as the codification of an international order based on orderly and sovereign states.

Since then, the different convulsions of the international order have all in essence been based on the principles established in Westphalia. The international order has been an order of orderly states. It is thus appropriate to talk about the long Westphalian era spanning the later part of the previous millennium.

In retrospect, we might say that there were two preconditions underlying this Westphalian order.

The first was that the evolution of technology and finance established a situation in which only states really could muster the resources to fundamentally threaten the existence or vital interests of another state. It thus took states to conduct war, and it accordingly also took states to make and uphold a peace.

The second was that the internal order of a state remained solely the concern of the ruler of that particular state. This was, of course, key to the Westphalian settlement since the religious wars that had torn Europe apart had often been based on interference by one ruler in the territories of other rulers in order to protect believers of a particular religious faith.

Although these principles have remained fundamental since then, they have, of course, not been universally respected.

For a while, the rise of well-organized naval piracy threatened the monopoly of power and force of nation-states. But when this threat developed beyond a certain level, intervention by states forced an end to the practice. The naval action against the so-called Barbary States of North Africa, which were semi-private pirating ventures, re-established the order, and also marked the first military appearance of the United States on the wider international scene.

Interventions designed to affect the internal order of states weren't entirely unknown either. There was a revolutionary impulse in the Napoleonic armies as they set out to first conquer and then reorder Europe, although the effort ended in failure, and reaction came to dominate the European scene for a long time thereafter. And the successive interventions in the decaying Ottoman Empire were more often than not motivated by an expressed desire primarily to protect its different Christian communities. As a result of this, there were even elaborate international arrangements for state- or nation-building in complex multiethnic areas like Macedonia a century ago.

The two great efforts of the 20th century to build a new international order—the League of Nations after the First World War and the United Nations after the Second—remained based on the Westphalian order of respect for the sovereignty of states, although other elements were gradually being added.

In the League of Nations, elaborate systems for the protection of minorities were built into the system, aimed at putting some limits on the sovereignty of the states in this important area. But when the United Nations was set up, minority issues were replaced by a not necessarily more concrete commitment to the protection of universal human rights. But in spite of its name, the organization was in reality an organization of states rather than nations, and most certainly not one of individuals. The opening line of its Charter—"We, the Peoples…"—should really be "We, the States…"

The Charter of the United Nations was specific in limiting the legitimate use of force in international affairs to either self-defense—Article 51—or such actions that had been authorized by the Security Council. The United Nations thus represented a continuation and codification of the Westphalian order, although it sought to place the relationship between the states within a firmer legal context.

During the decades of the Cold War, there is no doubt that we saw massive violations of the principles underlying the Charter of the United Nations. The Soviet Union was not averse to giving open or clandestine support to different so-called revolutionary movements around the world, and its establishment of a belt of satellite regimes in Central Europe in the 1940s through a series of coups d´etat was, of course, a gross violation of the principles of non-interference. When its forces invaded Hungary in 1956 and Czechoslovakia in 1968, they did so on pretexts that had no international legal validity whatsoever. Neither did the United States, on occasion, feel itself unnecessarily constrained by the limitations of international law when protecting its interests or engaging in what it considered the fight against the forces of communism.

It was thus after the fall of the Soviet Empire between 1989 and 1991 that hopes were ignited for a New World Order in which the United Nations and its legal system would come to true fruition. The marshalling of a great military coalition under the full authority of the United Nations to expel Iraq from Kuwait was only one part of what seemed to be an emerging new global order based on the primacy of the United Nations, cooperation between the major powers, and an increasing respect for international law.

But soon these hopes were dashed. We were confronted with a global situation where disorder was more dominant than order, and the Westphalian system came under attack and threat. During the last few years, we have seen both the two main pillars of the Westphalian order starting to crumble.

While the principle of state sovereignty was previously seen as sacrosanct, the combination of the NATO intervention in Kosovo in 1999 and the non-intervention by the international community in Rwanda in 1995 has led to an intense discussion about the right or duty to intervene in sovereign states in order to prevent massive violations of human rights.

And in contrast to the previously unchallenged dominance of the state in the international system, the September 2001 attacks against the United States illustrated the threat that the marriage between modern technologies and ancient hatreds can present to even the most powerful state. Small bands of dedicated individuals can now obtain the power to threaten the fundamental interests of the most powerful of states.

This, in its turn, has led to a debate on the right to intervene in order to preempt a threat of this sort from developing. The publication of the U.S. National Security Strategy a year after the devastating 2001 attack ignited a major international debate on the issue.

Although the attack on the Saddam Hussein regime in Iraq was justified in different ways, most importantly by Iraq's material breach of numerous resolutions of the UN Security Council,[1] it was the perception

---

[1] UN Security Resolution 1441, adopted unanimously, stated that "Iraq has been and remains in material breach of its obligations under relevant resolutions, including resolution 687." It also recalled that "in its resolution 687 the Council declared that a ceasefire would be based on the acceptance by Iraq on the provisions of that resolution, including the obligations on Iraq contained therein." In spite of this, Iraq was given "a final opportunity" to comply, and the Council recalled that the country "will face serious consequences as a result of its continued violations of its obligations."

that these breaches were part of a pattern of rapid development of weapons of mass destruction that gave the issue its urgency.

Taken together, these developments have led to a debate on whether we are on our way towards an international order that has firmly left the foundations of the previous Westphalian order behind. We might feel compelled to intervene for humanitarian reasons in cases where existing governments have collapsed or are clearly failing in their duty to protect their citizens, and we might feel the necessity to intervene when there are imminent and serious threats of destruction towards our societies that can't be handled otherwise.

Now, there is a need to look at both of these issues in the light of the lessons learned and to try to draw the appropriate conclusions.

In the United States, the doctrine of preemption announced in the National Security Strategy seems to command wide support[2] with the present debate focusing on whether a preemptive attack against Afghanistan should have been launched before September 11. In the European Union, the adoption in December 2003 of the European Security Strategy showed an awareness of the new challenges that the changed international security environment presents. Recently, the UN Secretary General appointed a high-level panel that has been asked to look into how the United Nations can be reformed in this new international situation. It is scheduled to report in December of this year.

# # #

This paper is written from a European as well as personal perspective. It is important to recognize that perspectives on these issues are different in different parts of the world.

Much of our theory of international relations, as well as principles underlying the global order, has been derived from the lessons learned during the centuries of war and peace on the European continent. A Eurocentric worldview is certainly to be avoided in today's world, but it

---

[2] It should be noted that the concept of preemption is not exclusive to the Bush administration. President Bush stated in his 2002 State of the Union address, that "when the threat is imminent, the nation has the right to conduct preemptive operations." Echoing this, Senator John Kerry recently said that "allies give us more hands in the struggle, but no President would ever let them tie our hands and prevent us from doing what must be done. As President, I will not wait for a green light from abroad when our safety is at stake." The difference in principle is not easy to detect.

remains a regrettable fact that conflicts in Europe twice during the last century led to wars that spanned the globe. Neither can we overlook the fact that most Europeans are only a generation away from the experience of wars that shattered the life of nations and families in a profound way. The word genocide had to be invented to describe a European 20th century reality.

These particular European experiences have colored the reaction of most Europeans in the ongoing international debate on these issues.

On the one hand, Europe has seen the consequences of regimes that violate fundamental principles of human rights perhaps more clearly than other parts of the world. A regime that attacks its own citizens sooner or later also risks attacking its neighbors. While representatives of many developing countries see doctrines of humanitarian intervention as little more than a new version of old-style colonialism, or even attempts to break up their states to prevent them from becoming too powerful, standing idly by as dictators or despots are running wild can never be a European policy after the experiences of the 20th century.

On the other side, Europe has experienced the devastating consequences of war more profoundly than have many other parts of the world. Within the living memory of large numbers of Europeans, millions of people have been slaughtered, towns and homes have been devastated and the inhabitants of entire regions have been forced to flee for their lives. War is not a concept treated easily after such experiences.

Preemption is not an entirely alien concept in European history. When Napoleon returned to Paris from Elba in 1815, the anti-Napoleonic coalition decided on and implemented a policy of preemption of the new threat that they were certain was coming. And it has often been argued that a strategy of preemption against Hitler when he reoccupied the Rhineland in 1936 could have caused his regime to fall.

But against this should be put the horrible historical legacy of the summer of preemption in 1914, when a chain of mutually reinforcing preemptive moves took Europe from the assassination in Sarajevo to world war in little more than a month. One has learned that doctrines of preemption can turn into a contagious disease with potentially devastating consequences.

Across the Atlantic, perspectives are often different. While "war" to an audience in the United States is something that happens elsewhere, with the brave soldiers going out and the "heroes" coming home soon thereafter, the word "war" has a distinctly different ring to a European ear. Here, "war" is something that sooner or later risks coming home to you with all of the devastating consequences numerous generations of

Europeans have seen.

Thus, while in the United States "war" is routinely proclaimed as part of a purely domestic agenda, in Europe the word could not officially be used for the de facto war over Kosovo in 1999.

With some simplification, the difference in attitudes between the United States and most of Europe on the issue of war can be seen as disagreement over the validity of the theories of Prussian military thinker Carl Von Clausewitz.

While his famous dictum that war is the continuation of politics by other means comes naturally in a state where one of the most important functions of the president is to be commander-in-chief of the armed forces, attitudes in Europe are different. On this side of the Atlantic, war isn't primarily seen as the continuation of politics, but rather as the failure of politics. Time after time, we have seen a readiness to go from diplomacy to armed action in the United States while there has been a substantial hesitancy in Europe. Geography as well as history has driven political attitudes in slightly different directions.

Although there is this significant cultural difference between Europe and the United States, there are also significant divergences within Europe. Both the United Kingdom and France maintain armed forces where important elements are geared for expeditionary warfare and interventions in more distant areas. Although a legacy from their colonial past, these capabilities have in recent years become increasingly important as part of different international stability operations.

Recent British intervention in support of the UN in Sierra Leone, and French intervention in Cote d'Ivoire in support of its authorities and with the endorsement of the UN, can be seen as examples of this. The commitment of both nations to retaining these capabilities is best illustrated by the UK decision to build two new aircraft carriers and the French decision to build a second new carrier. In both Paris and London, there is a Clausewitzian tendency stronger than in other European capitals, although still on a level well below that found in the political atmosphere of Washington.

But in spite of this, it must be recognized that there remains a significant difference between the strategic culture of the United States and what there is of a common strategic culture in the countries of the European Union.

# # #

The Westphalian international order was dominated by state threats against states, while the post-Westphalian order to a far larger extent is dominated by non-state threats, intrastate conflicts as well as a multitude of transnational challenges.

In the old order, threats to the security and survival of states almost invariably originated from other states. Until 1989, it was the threat of Soviet invasion that defined the security order in Europe.

Since then, weak and imploding states have turned out to be far more of a security challenge than strong and expanding ones at the same time as different transnational challenges have made their contribution to the reordering of the international system. The emergence of the organized forces of religious fundamentalist terrorism has added to these threats. We live in a profoundly changed global security environment.

This does not mean that old challenges have disappeared altogether. The series of wars in the Balkans demonstrated the continued strength of nationalist forces. In that case, they contributed to the breakup of existing state structures, while in others it can be envisaged that the same sentiments can fuel the flames leading to interstate aggression of a more conventional model.

It was the collapse of the old Socialist Federal Republic of Yugoslavia that led to the decade of war from 1991 in Slovenia to 2001 in Macedonia as one state structure after the other was challenged and old nationalist fears and passions were revived. As we started to struggle with the new challenges of a new international order, we were brutally reminded of the force that old issues and old challenges still have. In a world of new challenges, the Balkans served notice that the old ones must not be neglected.

And since 2001, we have become far more aware of the dangers that could originate from zones of chaos and disorder in the different parts of the world where we see fragile, failing or failed states.

These dangers come in different forms.

In the more extreme form, we have seen how zones outside the international state system can become havens for terrorist groups, with the al Qaeda takeover of parts of Taliban-run Afghanistan as the foremost example. In no less serious form, we have witnessed how such zones can become the origin of drugs that not only fuel local conflicts, but also finance vast networks of internationally organized crime and eventually lead to destructive dependence and death in the midst of our own society.

The cocaine market in America is as much fueled from the stateless areas within conflict-ridden Colombia as are the heroin markets of Europe from the stateless areas within post-conflict Afghanistan. When states fracture and collapse, we have also seen how this often triggers humanitarian catastrophes and leads to the eruption of cycles of violence that easily descend into tribal or national conflicts with the risk of genocide-like situations.

More often than not, we see these different developments reinforcing each other and creating negative spirals of increasingly dangerous character.

When a state starts to fail completely or in part, zones of chaos and lawlessness create opportunities both for extremist groups and for networks of organized criminality. These, in turn, extend over borders, often causing the cancer of chaos and instability to spread. Not infrequently, we see these developments associated with national or cultural links or divides that cover larger regions and act as transmission belts of chaos and conflict across state boundaries. Thus, there is not only the risk of grave violations of human rights, including genocide in extreme cases, but also of regional destabilization.

In whole or in part, this is what we have seen in the Balkans, in Central Asia connected with Afghanistan, the Great Lakes region of Africa as well as substantial parts of West Africa and the borderlands immediately south of the Sahara. But the same tendencies also exist in parts of the Caucasus, areas of the Andean region in Latin America, the Indonesian archipelago as well as the Philippines.

Not always related to these issues are those connected with the spread of the technologies of weapons of mass destruction. Although originating in sophisticated research laboratories, there is always the risk that these technologies will spread to areas of chaos and conflict.

While classic policies of deterrence might still work in preventing more or less rational state actors from using these weapons, such policies are of no use against dedicated terrorist groups, often motivated by a religious or political fundamentalism beyond rationality.

Thus, we are increasingly faced with the question of our right to intervene in one way or another in such situations, sometimes as part of our efforts to safeguard our own citizens, and sometimes as part of wider efforts to uphold more universal human values and avert more serious threats to global stability.

# # #

Intervention remains a charged word. To a large extent we are still politically programmed by an earlier age of more complete state sovereignty, when any sort of outside interference or intervention in the affairs of one state was to be avoided. The resistance to interference and intervention has its firm historical roots in the Westphalian order of sovereign, independent and well-ordered states.

But today we live in a world of increasing interdependence between states, and thus of de facto gradually reduced independence of states within the international system. When we speak about the accelerating process of globalization, we are at the same time speaking about an accelerating process of interdependence that step by step undermines the old independence of the sovereign states.

Gradually, the international system seeks to formalize this interdependence and create universally accepted instruments for what we might call "soft interventions" in the affairs of the different states. Nearly all major international institutions, and primarily those set up as part of the United Nations system or remaining from the League of Nations, have more or less elaborate instruments and systems for soft intervention. These can range from agreements that limit the freedom of action of states in different respects to more intrusive evaluation of state policies and recommendations on how they could be changed, to even more elaborate inspections and international decisions that have to be respected.

The more globalization proceeds and interdependence thus increases, the more we are likely to see these different forms of soft interventions. The different mechanisms of the World Trade Organization most definitely interfere in the internal lives of different states, the surveillance mechanisms of the International Monetary Fund have a power that is reinforced by the action of the international financial markets, and the different instruments of inspection and information exchange of the World Health Organization are as intrusive as they are necessary in an age where an infectious disease can travel the globe in just hours.

As this development accelerates in the coming decade, we could perhaps speak of a system where there is a continuum of interventions, ranging from the softest to the hardest, but all aiming at assuring that the different states don't deviate too much from the norms and values that underpin the evolving international system. In trying to secure common values, and react to threats against them, the global system would thus rely on an escalating ladder of instruments ranging from diplomacy and the force of public opinion at one end of the scale to hard military-dominated interventions in the extreme cases at the other.

To gradually extend the networks and structures of interdependence, integration and soft intervention is by no means uncontroversial. In Europe, there is a vigorous debate about how far the powers of the different common European institutions should be allowed to go. In the United States, there is often even less tolerance for the decrees of international institutions, although at the end of the day informed opinion normally comes to the conclusion that a United States inside the international order is better than one outside it. In other countries that consider themselves powers of some consequence, one often finds reactions not too dissimilar from those of the United States. On the recent controversial issue of the International Criminal Court, Russia, China and India do not accept its jurisdiction.

But more controversial than this gradual evolution of soft interventions is the question of the need for harder interventions, including the use of violence, in cases where it is obvious both that soft interventions are not enough and that the issues at stake are of particular importance from a wider global perspective.

A massive breakdown in preventing violations of human rights, a complete collapse of the willingness or ability of a state to help and assist its citizens, or a more or less imminent threat of both the spread and the use of weapons of mass destruction are all cases in which the question of hard intervention is immediately on the table. Kosovo, Somalia, Iraq or Haiti can be seen—irrespective of the merits of the individual cases—as examples of the issues and dilemmas with which we can be confronted.

The ideal scenario is for such a situation to be addressed by the Security Council, perhaps after having been brought to its attention by the Secretary-General, resulting in a resolution binding on all concerned, and mandating either the United Nations itself, or a coalition of the willing and able, to use force in order to assure compliance with the provisions of the resolution.

Despite all the disagreements over the past few years, there remains universal agreement that this is the preferred and best option in practically all of these situations. Such a course secures the legality of any action taken, giving it legitimacy and thereby increasing the chances of the hard intervention being successful in achieving the aims set. Thus, it seems likely that, in most cases in the future, taking the issue to the Security Council will remain among the first options considered when faced with situations like the ones described above. Indeed, this should be the rule.

It might be that the case for doing so would be strengthened even further if there were a possibility of changing the composition of the Security Council so as to reflect the realities of today rather than those of an increasingly distant past. But while over time it would make perfect sense for the European Union to become a permanent member of the Council, amalgamating the present British or French positions, as well as enlarging this group with powers like Japan, India or Brazil, the likelihood of this happening within the foreseeable future is very close to nil.

While it is useful to keep up the debate on the composition of the

Security Council, it seems futile to spend too much energy on it, and it is questionable whether a thus enlarged and reformed Council would be able to perform better than the one we actually have.

Irrespectively, we are likely to continue to be confronted with occasional situations in which states that start by bringing an issue to the attention of the Security Council decide at the end of the day to take action without its full authorization.

During recent decades, we have also seen numerous examples of states intervening militarily in other states without even seeking the sanction of the UN Security Council. India did so in East Pakistan in 1971, thus contributing to the creation of Bangladesh. Tanzania invaded Idi Amin's Uganda in 1978 and 1979, and Vietnam did the same to Cambodia during the same years. Although some humanitarian motives could be put forward for these interventions, they were primarily motivated by more traditional national concerns.

The more recent cases of Kosovo and Iraq are different from these in that the key debates prior to intervention took place in the Security Council. There was a fair degree of agreement on the issues at stake, but in the end there was a parting of ways when it came to authorizing hard intervention.

Experience shows that we must seek criteria broader than just the formal legal authority of the Security Council in order to assess whether a hard intervention should be undertaken. Experience also shows that there are several criteria of importance, and it is rare that all of them are met in every case.

# # #

When a hard intervention is contemplated, one should aim at fulfilling three different but interrelated criteria.

First, one should seek to assure its legality. Second, one should seek to broaden its legitimacy. And third, one should do the utmost to increase its chances of effectiveness in meeting the objectives set.

If, as in the recent cases of Kosovo and Iraq, the hard intervention does not fulfill all the criteria under international law, it is obviously deprived of a critical amount of legitimacy, which in turn makes it more difficult to achieve the third requirement of effectiveness in achieving the aims of the intervention.

But the relationship between these three requirements is by no means clear-cut. That an action is formally legal does not automatically assure it of the legitimacy that comes from being accepted as necessary by most of those affected by the intervention in question. And one can well contemplate interventions that are both legal and legitimate but which are most unlikely to achieve their stated goal.

For democracies, the legitimacy of hard interventions is a critically important issue. A democratic political system will simply not accept the burdens of a hard intervention if it is not seen as having legitimacy in one way or another. By far the best way of laying the groundwork for the legitimacy of an operation remains having it endorsed by the UN Security Council, thus taking away any discussion concerning the formal legality of the action.

But increasingly it is argued that some form of legitimacy can be given to a hard intervention in other ways than an explicit decision by the UN Security Council.

Some of these issues can be illustrated with the case of Kosovo.

Here, where there was substantially less legal foundation for hard intervention in Security Council resolutions than in the case of Iraq, it was argued that some legitimacy for the air campaign was given by the decisions of the North Atlantic Council, bringing together most of the democracies of North America and Western Europe. But the most important contribution to the legitimacy of the air campaign was undoubtedly the television images of the nearly one million refugees fleeing the province during the fighting. The intervention was seen as a necessary response to a humanitarian disaster and ethnic cleansing.

But the roots of the military intervention were different. The threat of the use of air power had been introduced in order to force the Milosevic regime into accepting a draft peace agreement. While the threat of the use of force is explicitly prohibited under the UN Charter, it had undoubtedly gained a certain legitimacy when Kofi Annan had returned from Baghdad in 1998 claiming that "diplomacy backed by force" had brought the success that he saw as having been achieved.

This is less of a problem when the threat works than when it does not. In the latter case, the original threat is often translated into an issue of the credibility of the issuer of the threat, and one risks navigating a slippery slope in which the purpose of the threatened military action evolves into something very different.

In the Kosovo case, Milosevic was not ready to give in to threats, and issues of credibility immediately came into play. This gained added weight since the threat to bomb Milosevic had been a key part of the successful efforts in persuading the Kosovo Albanian side to accept the draft agreement. A threat that had been introduced as a diplomatic tool thus quickly became something very different when that diplomacy failed.

When, as a consequence of the credibility issue, NATO initiated the air campaign, it was motivated by the need to avert an imminent humanitarian disaster. Although there had been brutal fighting in Kosovo, and a substantial number of people had been displaced, fighting had been relatively limited, and there were as yet no streams of refugees crossing the borders.

The air campaign proved to be far longer and more complicated than those taking part in the decisions had obviously anticipated. Large-scale fighting immediately flared up on the ground, and when the flood of refugees started coming, it soon become clear that air power was an instrument with only a very limited possibility of influencing ground fighting.

After nearly two months of an air campaign that gradually concentrated less on influencing the situation on the ground in Kosovo than inflicting strategic damage on Serbia, fighting came to an end with an agreement that affirmed the sovereignty of Yugoslavia over Kosovo while placing it under a UN administration, but otherwise failed to address any of the core issues of the conflict. If the threat of military intervention had been introduced as an instrument to achieve a peace settlement, it produced a situation where this looked more elusive than ever. It was somewhat ironic that, while the military intervention had been initiated against the background of a deeply split Security Council, the military campaign could be brought to an end only by the key members of the Security Council coming together again to agree on a political strategy.[3]

The Kosovo war also illustrates the complexities of the third criterion that should be used when trying to analyze possible hard interventions. As the aim of the use of force was described in very different ways as the conflict progressed, the ultimate objective of the intervention was also described in very different ways.

The core of the conflict was the question of sovereignty over the province of Kosovo. The Serb sovereignty over the area was militarily challenged by the KLA fighters, and they made little secret of their aim of freeing it from Serb control and establishing either a new independent state of Kosovo or joining up the different Albanian lands in some sort of state structure. Throughout the conflict, representatives of NATO countries

---

[3] It is striking how it is the very immediate, often military aims that dominate Wesley Clark's book *Waging Modern War* (New York: Public Affairs, 2001) while the political and more long-term issues are nearly completely absent. There is, for example, no mention of the aims of the KLA and the compatibility, or incompatibility, of these with NATO aims.

clearly dissociated themselves from these aims, and, in the text that was presented to Milosevic and that led to the withdrawal of Serb forces from the province and the setting up of an interim UN administration, the sovereignty of Yugoslavia over Kosovo was reaffirmed in even stronger terms than had been the case in the different attempts at political settlement prior to the open conflict.

As for the humanitarian aims of the intervention, the months after saw the return of close to a million refugees and displaced persons, almost all of them of Albanian nationality, but also the more or less forced expulsion of up to a quarter of a million non-Albanians after the arrival of NATO forces and the UN. Thus, if the aim was the protection of the Kosovo Albanians, that aim was met, but if the aim was protection of human and minority rights in more general terms, and an end to ethnic cleansing, the result was little more than turning the tables in a centuries-old conflict.

If previously Albanians had been a repressed minority in Serbia, now Serbs were a repressed minority in Kosovo. As long as the core issue of the conflict has not been settled, and the consequences of the settlement for the wider regional order are unclear, it will be difficult to draw up a balance sheet as to the efficacy of the Kosovo intervention in meeting more than some of the most immediate aims.[4]

What the Kosovo example illustrates is that we should give far more attention to the possible effectiveness as well as long-term political goals of different hard interventions. Although the decision-making process is often driven by short-term considerations, it is the long-term consequences of these interventions with which we must live, and by which they will eventually be judged.

Interventions to protect a national minority, as was the case in Kosovo, are sometimes fraught with other dangers. We should not overlook that concern for the rights of minorities could be used as a pretext for quite different motives. That Hitler used the provisions for the protection of minorities in the League of Nations system in his campaigns against both Czechoslovakia and Poland, claiming that the rights of the German minorities were infringed upon, shows how real the dangers could be. In the Russian political debate, there have been voices claiming that Russia

---

[4] It is sometimes claimed that the NATO intervention was key to the toppling of the Milosevic regime in Serbia and that this should be part of the balance sheet. But the short-term effect of the intervention was rather to strengthen the regime. Milosevic fell because of his own mistake of calling the September 2000 presidential elections and having to engineer a massive vote fraud in order to win. He failed.

should have a right to unilateral interventions in neighboring countries in order to protect the interests of the approximately 25 million Russians living there.

It seems necessary to establish some sort of rule that interventions of this sort can never be seen as either legal or legitimate if not preceded by, at the least, substantial and repeated debate in the UN Security Council. This would seem to provide a safeguard against the misuse of interventions to protect minorities or otherwise suffering populations, since it will always be possible for the Security Council as such, or a majority of its members, to take a position explicitly depriving an intervention of its legality. This did not happen in either the Kosovo or Iraq cases. If it were to be repeated in another case, it is difficult to see that such an operation would have any legitimacy whatsoever.

The intervention in Iraq in 2003 can also serve as an illustration of the importance of the three criteria of legality, legitimacy and effectiveness.

Here, the legal foundations for intervention were clearer than in the case in Kosovo in 1999, but the legitimacy of the operation far less clear among public opinion either in Europe or in the Arab or wider Muslim world.

As to the ultimate efficacy of the operation, it is, of course, much too early to judge. This is complicated by the fact that the aims of the intervention have been described in different ways, from enforcing the resolutions of the UN Security Council, securing "regime change" in Iraq, to stimulating a fundamental reform of the different regimes of the Greater Middle East. While non-compliance with Security Council resolutions is no longer an issue, the ultimate effect of the intervention on the future of Iraq and the political evolution of the wider Arab world, including the issue of Palestine, will take a long time to assess.

In an even more profound way than Kosovo, the example of Iraq has demonstrated that military intervention is just the first phase of a prolonged period of heavy involvement in the economic and political affairs of the region or the country in question. If one order or regime is destroyed by military intervention, ultimate responsibility for building a different and better order or regime often rests with the power responsible for the intervention.

The sometimes popular phrase "regime change" hides both the comparatively easy first phase of "regime destruction" and the much more complex and demanding phase of "regime construction." If this second phase is not successful, the risk is that the attempted regime change results in a situation of chaos and disorder—"regime absence"—or a situation in which a fragile regime has to be kept from failing completely by an extensive international support mechanism.[5]

Particularly in the U.S. debate, the notion of "regime change" has been introduced as a way of handling the threat of the spread of weapons of mass destruction. While the Clinton administration spoke about "rogue regimes," and did not shy away from the concept of regime change in these cases, the Bush administration introduced the "axis of evil" encompassing the regimes in Pyongyang, Teheran and Baghdad.

Subsequent events have demonstrated a reality that is more complex. The post-war operations in Iraq, only a medium-size country, have tied down such a high portion of U.S. ground force units that the United States has turned into a de facto weak global power in relation to other threats and situations that might occur. Whether imposed regime change would ever have been considered a realistic option in other cases or not, the reality is that at present there aren't the forces available to do it.

Preemptive use of military power to stop the development, deployment or use of weapons of mass destruction is not a new concept. During the Cuban missile crisis, President Kennedy contemplated preemptive air strikes against the ongoing deployment of Soviet medium-range missiles.[6] It is also highly likely that the Soviet leadership at some point looked into the possibility of preemptive strikes in order to prevent China from gaining an operational nuclear capability. And preemptive strikes were among the options considered by the Clinton administration when dealing with the North Korean situation prior to the 1994 agreement.

In all of these cases, detailed deliberations have shown that the risks associated with the preemptive option were greater than the possible benefits. In each of these cases, there was never any certainty that all of the weapons or facilities could be destroyed, while the risk of counter-action using assets that had not been hit was very substantial.

The only case of actual preemptive use of military power against a program of weapons of mass technologies was the June 1981 Israeli air

---

[5] In the case of Iraq, this can be illustrated by the warning by the Director of the Defense Intelligence Agency to the Select Committee of Intelligence of the U.S. Senate on February 24, 2004: "Iraq has the potential to serve as a training ground for the next generation of terrorists where novice recruits develop their skills, junior operatives hone their operational and planning capabilities, and relations mature between individuals and groups as was the case during the Soviet occupation of Afghanistan and extremist operations in the Balkans." If this were to happen, it could be argued that the intervention has failed at least one of the important objectives stated for it.

[6] See the excellent discussions in Lawrence Freedman's acclaimed *Kennedy's Wars* (New York: Oxford University Press, 2000).

strike against the Osiraq reactor in Iraq. Roundly condemned as a violation of international law,[7] the strike was a short-term success in that it did destroy the reactor. The overall effect was to drive the Iraqi nuclear effort in other directions, and had it not been for the decision of Saddam Hussein to launch the invasion of Kuwait before he had access to nuclear weapons, there is little doubt that Iraq would have been successful with its modified secret nuclear program.

The success of the Osiraq strike is thus somewhat debatable. It complicated and delayed the Iraqi nuclear efforts, but not much more than that. In the end, it was only the stupidity of Saddam Hussein in launching the Kuwait invasion too early that prevented Iraq from acquiring a nuclear capability.

If experience prior to the Iraq war thus had demonstrated the tactical as well as strategic difficulties with preemptive strikes against nations seen as harboring plans to develop weapons of mass destruction, the Iraq war has, of course, further highlighted some of these. In all the previous cases, preemptive action was not undertaken in the absence of sufficiently reliable intelligence as to location, at the moment of strike, of every component of the alleged program or capability that needed taking out.

The Iraq war has certainly further underlined the limitations of even the most advanced intelligence gathering efforts in cases like these. Here, there was a failure both of tactical intelligence on the location of individual facilities, and of strategic intelligence about the overall nature of the threat.[8]

Strategies of preemptive use of military force must be based on intelligence capabilities far more reliable than those recently demonstrated. While the run-up to the Iraq war is an example of a threat exaggerated, we should also note that intelligence for a long time seems to have underestimated both the clandestine nuclear sales network in Pakistan as well as the nuclear and missile ambitions of Libya.

If an attempt to apply the criteria of "effectiveness" to hard interventions directed at weapons of mass destruction has thus

---

[7] The UN Security Council, including the United States, condemned the attack as "a clear violation of the Charter of the United Nations and the norms of international conduct."

[8] One glaring example of a tactical intelligence failure concerns the alleged bunker complex that caused the plans for the initiation of the war to be altered so that it could be attacked after reliable intelligence indicated that Saddam Hussein was hiding there. After the war, the location was revealed to be nothing more than an open field with big bomb craters. Bob Woodward's *Plan of Attack* (New York: Simon & Schuster, 2004) gives the details of an extensive intelligence effort that in the end proved unreliable.

demonstrated some of the inherent difficulties, the picture is not much clearer when it comes to hard interventions in order to safeguard basic human rights.

Here it might be useful to make a distinction between short-term and long-term effects. If there is an imminent threat of a massive violation of human rights, a hard intervention will have to occur very fast and very effectively in order to prevent this from happening. At the same time, there is always the more long-term possibility that a hard intervention to change the regime of a nation or a region might produce a better situation in terms of human rights and basic humanitarian conditions.

Srebrenica is often used as an example to describe the failures of international efforts in this area, and can also serve as an illustration of the difficulties.

The fall of the Srebrenica enclave in Eastern Bosnia in July 1995 came as a surprise to the international community, and the subsequent massacre of thousands taken prisoners was not reliably known until weeks after it had taken place. Apart from the fact that it is highly doubtful that sufficient forces could have been brought to the remote Bosnian location of Srebrenica sufficiently fast to make a difference, there was neither intelligence nor other information that pointed either to the imminent fall of the enclave or the massacres that followed. Even if forces are available, it is difficult to intervene against the unknown.[9]

Kosovo illustrates other limitations. Here, air power was singularly ineffective in changing what was happening on the ground during the nearly three months of the campaign. The Serb forces left Kosovo in good order and with more intact equipment than NATO intelligence has assessed they had at the beginning of the air campaign. If there was any effect on human rights violations in Kosovo itself during the nearly three months of air campaign, it was in all likelihood distinctly negative. Thus, air power alone is a most dubious instrument of intervention when it comes to protecting human rights or preventing humanitarian emergencies.

The most frequently quoted example of a failure of the international community to intervene is the Rwanda genocide in 1994. A UN mission was already on the ground, with its leader trying to bring attention to the

---

[9] Even after the fall of the enclave, and the humiliation of the international community this represented, it was difficult to mobilize action. France asked the United States for help with helicopters in order to get an assault force to the area, but the request was turned down as such an operation was deemed as too dangerous.

risk of genocide and calling for a battalion of reinforcements to prevent this. But the attention of the UN Secretariat as well as the Security Council was elsewhere—the Mogadishu debacle in Somalia had occurred in October of the preceding year—and the policy decided upon was instead a dramatic reduction of the UN presence in Rwanda. It is estimated that 800,000 Tutus lost their lives in the genocide between April and June of that year.[10]

For any intervention to satisfy the criteria of effectiveness, it must be both timely and firm in its initial phase and prepared to stay the course for possibly a very prolonged period in order to assure that the goals set are really met.

For the debate on humanitarian interventions, the report in December 2001 by the International Commission on Intervention and State Sovereignty has been most important. Its central thesis that state sovereignty is dependent on a "responsibility to protect" paves the way for a right, perhaps even an obligation, for the international community to intervene if a state manifestly does not live up to its responsibility to protect its population, and other means to affect the situation are not available.

Using this concept, a hard intervention in a situation like this must be seen as a transfer of the "responsibility to protect" from the state structures of the area in question to the intervening authority of the international community. That responsibility then rests with the intervening authority or coalition until such time that state- or institution-building efforts have led to a situation that the "responsibility to protect" can safely be transferred back to more indigenous authorities.

If we see humanitarian intervention as an enforced transfer of the "responsibility to protect" to the intervening body, this has the advantage of focusing more attention on the task of living up to that responsibility until such time as it can be transferred back again than on the short-term intervention itself. Such a focus on the effectiveness over a longer time in ensuring the success of the intervention could help in focusing planning

---

[10] Former U.S. Ambassador to the UN Richard Holbrooke made a forceful point on this issue in the *Washington Post*, April 4, 2004: "Had the Security Council agreed to the UN commander's request and sent more troops, I believe, as do most observers, that at least half the deaths, if not more, could have been prevented. Instead, when the United Nations withdrew, the genocide exploded... It was not 'the UN'—that tall building on New York's East River, overflowing with diplomatic talk—that decided to pull out. It was the leading nations of the world, speaking through their ambassadors in New York."

and preparation efforts on the essential post-intervention tasks more often than has been the case thus far.

The demands that this approach puts on the international community should not be underestimated. If there were, for example, a requirement to make hard interventions and transfers of "responsibility to protect" in every case with a degree of violence similar or higher to Kosovo pre-March 1999, the capability of the international community, both in respect of quick early interventions and long-term peacekeeping and state-building, would very soon be exhausted.

Thus, while we should be aware of the risks of setting criteria that will prevent us from intervening in acute situations of different sorts, we should also be aware of the risks of an "intervention overload" quickly leading to an "intervention fatigue" in the leading countries. Over time, this might turn out to be just as detrimental to the values and interests we are seeking to protect.

###

In December 2003, the countries of the European Union came together in agreeing on a European Security Strategy, thus making their first attempt to develop a common strategic culture and set out the policies to be pursued in the post-Westphalian area. It is expected that this European Security Strategy will be regularly revisited and reviewed.[11]

The European Security Strategy starts from the assumption that large-scale aggression against any member state is now improbable, and that the Union is instead faced with new threats that are more diverse, less visible and less predictable. Of these, the strategy mentions in particular terrorism, proliferation of weapons of mass destruction, regional conflicts, state failure and organized crime.

In discussing the different threats, the strategy underlines the dynamic nature of these and stresses that accordingly "we should be ready to act before a crisis occurs." It stresses that "conflict prevention and threat prevention cannot start too early."

From a European perspective, a key goal is to develop the instruments of the United Nations as the core of a system of "effective multilateralism."

The addition of the word "effective" is a subtle shift of obvious political significance. It is not multilateralism for its own sake, but multilateralism for better effectiveness in reaching the stated objectives. And in this also lies a commitment to constantly review and reform different multilateral instruments in order to increase their effectiveness.

---

[11] *A secure Europe in a better world: European Security Strategy* (Paris: The European Union Institute for Security Studies, 2003).

Within or outside this framework, the strategy stresses the need "to develop a strategic culture that fosters early, rapid, and when necessary, robust intervention."

Much remains in order to develop the instruments and policies needed to transform the European Security Strategy into more operational reality. But it should not be overlooked that its adoption represents a quantum leap in the attitude of the countries of the European Union to these issues. Previous feeble attempts at formulating a distinct European security strategy have all come to nothing. It required the twin trauma of September 11 and the disarray of the reaction to the Iraq war to mobilize the political will to make it possible.

In three areas, in particular, it will be necessary to develop the institutions and policies of the European Union.

The first is to develop the instruments of analysis and policy prediction so that potential crisis or conflicts can better be predicted, thus making it possible both to take European preventive action of whatever sort might be required and to alert the international community as a whole to the issue in question.

The second is to develop the instruments of increasingly harder, but still fundamentally soft, interventions in order to deal with the issue or challenge in question. Here, numerous approaches could be taken. In many cases, different parts of the UN system will be of critical importance, while in others political "coalitions of the willing" might be mobilized in order to try to address a particular issue.

And the third is obviously to have the means also for the extreme cases when a hard intervention, in the end, might seem to be the only alternative left, providing it can meet a reasonable mix of the three criteria outlined above. Here the issue is less about providing the military forces for initial expeditionary warfare and more about assuring that the manpower and money are available for the follow-up mission that will decide the success or the failure of the intervention in question.

While the quantum leap of the adoption of the European Security Strategy has been taken, it is obvious that much remains. There is no denying that the strategic cultures of different European nations—sharpened by their respective historical experience—sometimes differ substantially, and that it will take a number of challenges until we see the firm emergence of the common strategic culture on which the European Security Strategy must be based. In our world of today, however, these challenges might come faster than most people believe.

Of the recent experiences that contribute to the gradual shaping of this common strategic culture, Operation Artemis in the Bunia area of the

Democratic Republic of Congo in the summer of 2004 is of particular significance. Here the EU answered a call from the UN for the rapid deployment of a robust force to cover the critical time until regular UN peacekeeping force could be deployed. Using national units and relying on national command assets (French), a multinational battalion-sized battle group was rapidly deployed to the Congo and exited the area after having fulfilled its mission, handing over to the deployed UN force. Without Operation Artemis, mass slaughter and killing might well have occurred in the area.

This operation has led both to the setting up of a reinforced capability for planning military missions within the Secretariat of the Council of the European Union and to the plans to create seven to nine battalion-sized battle groups that could be deployed to any given location within 15 days. It is not only the ability that was demonstrated in Operation Artemis that has driven this, but also the recognition that if effective action should be taken to avert a threatening genocide or humanitarian disaster, it is only swift action that has any possibility of success. In the Rwandan case, a deployment of a force of this size within this time frame would in all probability have prevented most— if not all—of the killing which occurred.

As the European Union gradually develops these more robust intervention capabilities, it will be able to act more effectively, primarily in support of actions authorized by the UN Security Council, but conceivably also in situations where European interests or values are seen as directly threatened. But where a clear-cut mandate from the Security Council for one reason or another is not possible, trying to lay down too strict rules in advance for what type of missions could be launched is a futile exercise—reality is likely to continue to outstrip our fantasy.

Parallel to the development of these military battle groups, it seems important that the European Union develop the concept of political intervention groups to prevent different conflicts or to resolve them well before a hard intervention becomes necessary. I use the term political intervention groups since it is perfectly feasible that the core groups executing different policies will be different, although operating within the same policy framework and to a large extent utilizing the evolving machinery of the Common Foreign and Security Policy to coordinate their action while keeping the other member countries fully in the picture.

It is easy to see that the United Kingdom and France, in view of both their positions on the UN Security Council and their diplomatic and military capabilities, as well as Germany, in view of its political and economic weight, will be more involved in these groups than most other EU member countries. Nevertheless, fears for the emergence of an exclusive triumvirate to speak for Europe are in all probability grossly overblown. In the past, we have seen Italy take a leadership role on an issue like Albania in the very successful Operation Alba intervention in that country in April and August 1997, and few would doubt that Spain is likely to be a key partner in any policy affecting either Latin America or the Maghreb countries.

What will be needed is a more coherent capability to analyze different emerging challenges and to shape the policies that could prevent them from bursting into open conflicts. There is also the need for more flexible instruments of informal diplomacy, as well as for more coherent policy support to the increasingly demanding state-building operations that will be undertaken across the globe. In most cases, the European component in them will be substantial, and it is thus appropriate that the European Union develops a more comprehensive approach to these issues.

It is against this background that I have previously argued for the establishment of a European Institute of Peace, bringing important governmental as well as non-governmental resources in these areas together under one roof, and thus facilitating a better common understanding of the different problems, a sometimes more informal way of handling them, and a more coherent policy approach to extremely demanding state-building tasks. [12]

In addition to developing its own capabilities in all of these areas, the European Union could assist in the development of the capabilities of other regional organizations. This applies in particular to the African Union. The initiative by the European Commission to set up an African Peacekeeping Facility to help in financing both the training and the deployment of regional African peacekeeping forces is an important step that shows great promise for the future.

Great importance must continue to be attached to the cooperative relationship between NATO and the European Union. Under the so-called Berlin Plus arrangements, the EU has already undertaken a minor

---

[12] A somewhat related proposal to set up a European Foundation for Good Governance was recently put forward by Mark Leonard and Richard Gowan in *Global Europe: Implementing the European Security Strategy* (Brussels: The British Council Brussels and The Foreign Policy Centre, 2004). In the United States, the U.S. Institute for Peace as well as the National Endowment for Democracy fulfill much the same roles as intended for these two European institutions. There is no doubt that the ability to deal with different global issues would improve if there were also more focused European efforts in these respects. The existing EU Institute for Security Studies fulfills different tasks.

peacekeeping operation in Macedonia and is now scheduled to take over in Bosnia after the completion of the NATO mission there.

It should be recognized, however, that many of the issues we are likely to be confronted with are likely to require a more multi-faceted approach than can be offered by a security organization alone. NATO will continue to be the default option for robust peace and stability operations, but they must take place within a political framework that also utilizes all the other peace-, stability- and state-building instruments at the disposal of the European Union.

The European Union neither has nor will have the ambition to emerge as a global strategic player on a par with the United States. It will always lack the completeness of the global strategic view, and its assets, primarily in the harder parts of the military spectrum, will always be more limited. Notwithstanding this, it is both desirable and likely that, as part of the efforts to meet the new global challenges, the European Union will develop both the new strategic culture that the European Security Strategy calls for and the different instruments necessary to put that strategic culture to concrete operational use.

As this happens, the prospects for handling the new global challenges are bound to improve.

# # #

As we confront the new challenges, three tasks should be placed in focus, the first of which is to recognize the magnitude of the challenges with which we are confronted. If the fundamental pillars of the Westphalian system have eroded or even collapsed, we are likely to be in a prolonged and uncertain period of transition to an emerging post-Westphalian international order.

It will take time for this order to find its shape. But based on our experience so far, it is likely to be based less on the independence and more on the interdependence between states and societies, less on national sovereignty and more on sovereignty in different layers, less on non-intervention than on permanent intervention, and more on networks than on nations.[13]

We must handle the emerging new dominance of the politics of identity, in contrast to the politics of ideology in the past, in a world of rapidly accelerating globalization and of the ongoing scientific and technological revolution.

---

[13] This later point is argued by Anne-Marie Slaughter in her *A New World Order* (Princeton, Princeton University Press, 2004).

It is little more than a decade ago since Samuel Huntington issued his stark warning that we were heading towards "the clash of civilizations and the remaking of world order."[14] A decade is a short period, but it is easy to see that he was more right than wrong, although the dominant clashes might well be within, rather than between, civilizations, with the escalating struggle between the idea of reform and the urge of reaction inside Islam as the dominating "civilizational" issue affecting the structure of the international order.

It is too early to judge how profound this "civilizational" conflict will be in the years and decades ahead. That we are faced with a totalitarian jihad with profound implications is beyond doubt, but it is far from clear how the balance between the forces of reform and reaction will develop in the different parts of the Muslim world in the years ahead.

A possible parallel is what happened in Europe half a millennium ago as the Reformation spread across the then Christian world, upsetting the political order and ushering in an era of confrontation that ended only with the Westphalian settlement of 1648. But it was a long and turbulent time between Martin Luther nailing his theses on the church door in Wittenberg in 1517 and that settlement.

At the same time as the battle for the hearts and minds of the Muslim world goes on, other forces of disruption are reshaping the global landscape. The accelerating process of globalization brings the prospect of both prosperity and freedom to hundreds of millions of people across the world, as we have seen in success from Shanghai to Santiago during the past decades.

But at the same time this process disrupts established patterns, challenges cultures and provokes resistance. The accelerating interdependence also fuels the rise of the politics of identity, with its possible destructive consequences.

In this volatile world of dynamic threats, the United States has emerged as the dominant power par excellence, with a military budget that equals what most other nations spend together, and with a global reach and space dominance that no one can even think of rivaling.

But this is only part of the story. At the same time as this is happening, this United States feels more insecure than perhaps at any time in modern history and is becoming increasingly aware of the very real limitations of its own powers. It might have unrivalled control of outer space, but it is certainly no superpower in the back streets of Baghdad. It finds its army

---

[14] Originally he laid out his thesis in "A Clash of Civilizations?," *Foreign Affairs,* Summer 1993, and then expanded it in *Clash of Civilizations and the Remaking of World Order* (New York: Simon & Schuster, 1996).

desperately overstretched and must note that popular opinion in states and regions of key importance for the future is turning increasingly against it.[15]

The paradox of the present situation is that the United States is an extreme superpower in relation to the other powers, but certainly not in relation to the challenges it is confronted with in large areas of the world.

If we did not have the United Nations, statesmen of all countries would certainly be busy trying to set it up. There are assuredly differences in the degree to which it is seen as the key instrument for handling the different global challenges, but only the most extreme would challenge the notion that we need an effective instrument of inclusive multinationalism like the United Nations.

The Secretary-General has recently set up a High-Level Panel on Threats, Challenges and Changes to study global security threats and recommend necessary changes.[16] It is due to report in December 2004.

It is less likely that the Panel will recommend sweeping changes to the basic structure that was agreed on in San Francisco in 1945. Attempts to rewrite the Charter, or to alter the composition of key institutions, however worthy these efforts might be, are unlikely to lead to more than prolonged and ultimately futile diplomatic battles that risk diverting attention from what really can and ought to be done.

The United Nations is an organization in need of reform because the United Nations is an organization very much needed in the present global situation. There is a constant need to reform and improve its political, peacekeeping as well as humanitarian operations, and to make certain that the full panoply of international organizations belonging to or related to the UN family operates with common goals.

The Millennium Development Goals, agreed to by the Millennium Summit in 2000, are a most important attempt to focus multilateral as well as national attempts towards common goals of obvious global significance. Although one should be careful in not overloading the system

---

[15] Support for the U.S. war against terrorism in large parts of the world is low, ranging from 56 percent in Kuwait to 2 percent among Palestinians and Jordanians. Support for America has dropped in most of the Muslim world. Favorable ratings in Morocco declined from 77 percent in 2000 to 27 percent in spring of 2004 and in Jordan from 25 percent in 2002 to only 5 percent in 2004 (Pew Research Center, March 16, 2004). The percentage of Saudis expressing confidence in the United States dropped from 63 percent in May 2000 to 11 percent in October 2003.

[16] Set up in November 2003. Former Thai Prime Minister Anand Panyarachun heads the 15-member panel.

with a multitude of complicated commitments, assuring little more than the neglect of them all, it is useful to occasionally bring major elements of the international community together in support of common goals like these. Although bodies like the G-8 or the G-20 are important in calling attention to different issues, there is no alternative to anchoring processes like these in the UN system.

After a period in which the organization came in for much criticism, we have now entered a phase in which the peacekeeping operations of the UN are again expanding very fast. At the time of this writing, the UN had approximately 48,000 troops deployed, but this figure is likely to increase to approximately 70,000 troops before the end of 2004. The UN missions in the Democratic Republic of Congo and Liberia have recently expanded, a mission in Cote d'Ivoire is starting up, and further missions are likely in Burundi, Haiti and Sudan.[17]

These UN missions come on top of even larger missions undertaken by different coalitions in other areas. In the Balkans, NATO is still responsible for substantial stability operations in both Kosovo and Bosnia, with the mid-March upsurge in ethnic violence in the former making any plans for further reductions impossible. In Afghanistan, NATO has taken over responsibility for the International Security Assistance Force (ISAF), primarily around Kabul, while a substantially larger U.S. force operates with a different mandate in the country. In Iraq, initial plans to slim down the U.S. troop presence to approximately 30,000 soldiers after the war have proved utterly unrealistic, and most observers would agree that present total force levels are still insufficient to create a secure framework for a successful political process.

In all these cases, we are confronted with complex state-building operations of which the attempt to establish a secure environment is only the necessary beginning. Be it in West Africa, the Great Lakes region or the vast post-Ottoman area that includes both former Yugoslavia and present day Iraq, the tasks are of a magnitude that will require vast resources and firm commitment for many years to come.

Based on the so-called Brahimi Report, the UN has improved its system of managing peacekeeping operations. The Brahimi Report was, however, issued in a period in which the concept of nation- or state-building was heavily contested, and in a diplomatic way steered clear of practically all of the very demanding challenges that such tasks will involve. Apart from

---

[17] Briefing by UN Under Secretary-General for Peacekeeping Operations Jean-Marie Guéhenno to the Special Committee on Peacekeeping Operations, March 24, 2004.

some vague words about what it referred to as peace-building, it did not address what is increasingly turning out to be the major task that most of the rapidly expanding UN and other multinational operations are now confronted with.

This is no longer sufficient. It is neither narrow peacekeeping, nor undefined so-called nation-building, but concrete state-building, that will have to be the focus of most of these operations in the years and decades ahead. The UN must go beyond what the Brahimi Report was able to say, draw on the lessons that have been learned in the past and see if it can evolve into the international community's default mechanism for state-building operations in key areas of the world.

In a world in which many of the threats to global stability and security are coming from fragile, failing or failed states, the importance of state-building or state-reforming capabilities for global stability might be compared with the importance of nuclear deterrence for stability during the decades of the Cold War.

It is realistic to expect that the European Union over time will be ready to take responsibility for these kinds of efforts in its immediate "near abroad," and it cannot be excluded that there will be cases where the United States will prefer to take the political lead as is the case in Iraq today. But given the number of operations that we are likely to see in the years to come, it remains the United Nations that will be mandated to undertake most of them. Thus, the reinforcement of its capabilities in this area is of critical importance to global security in the decades ahead.

This will never be possible if these efforts do not have solid support from the key international actors. I have already dealt with the different efforts underway inside the European Union, as well as with the further steps that are necessary. It is worth noting that it is with the support of the United States that the present, almost unprecedented, expansion of peacekeeping operations is taking place. From a beginning in the UN operation in Cambodia, to the present difficult situation in Iraq, we also see a more active and important role played by Japan on these issues. Japan has also taken an active interest in the political efforts both in the Balkans and in Afghanistan.

But efforts in areas of fragile, failing or failed states must not be restricted to heavy state-building operations of this sort. It is worth noting the efforts undertaken in recent years by the UN Development Program to develop programs to improve governance and establish different indicators that could warn against developments that might threaten the stability of states or regions. While not intrusive in themselves, these efforts can provide important support to other international efforts.[18] The emphasis on issues of good governance and reform by the UNDP is worth supporting and developing further.

In a large number of other areas, it will be important to develop the different multilateral instruments of soft intervention to handle the new challenges.

When the Security Council adopted its resolution 1373 condemning the terrorist attacks of September 11, 2001, it took the important step of declaring that "such acts, like any act of international terrorism, constitute a threat to international peace and security" and immediately thereafter reaffirmed "the inherent right of individual or collective self-defense." This resolution established the Counter-Terrorism Committee (CTC), composed of the members of the Security Council. Although CTC has been beset by problems, it has become a key instrument in giving legitimacy to the global efforts against terrorism. Further steps to strengthen and improve the functioning of the CTC must be discussed.

Other areas where instruments must be reinforced are all those related to proliferation of technologies of mass destruction. The International Atomic Energy Agency Additional Protocol, with its more intrusive inspections, should form part of the core commitment required of states that are part of the system. There are also important discussions underway on the possibility of further control of the entire nuclear fuel cycle, thus making it possible to take a positive look at the increased use of nuclear power to meet the escalating electricity needs in different parts of the world. Consideration should be given to making the Proliferation Security Initiative more formally a part of the multilateral system, although one should not underestimate the important role of informal groups like the Nuclear Suppliers Group or the Wassenaar Group when it comes to controlling critical technologies.

If the first conclusion relates to the need to understand the magnitude of the change in which we are now engaged, and the second to the importance of improving and developing the international instruments for managing interdependence and handling state-building tasks, the third relates to the need to improve the ability of different actors—not least the Trilateral countries—to act within this reformed international system.

---

[18] The *Arab Human Development Report 2002* produced by the United Nations Development Program and the Arab Fund for Economic and Social Development (New York: United Nations Publications, 2002) presents an excellent example. It quickly became the basis for wide-ranging debate about the need for reforms in the Arab world.

It is easy to see that the Trilateral world faces major deficiencies in what we might call 3D spending and efforts—*diplomacy, development* and *defense*. If we add together the shares of our GDPs spent on 3D efforts for global stability, we are likely to find that they were lower at the beginning of the new century than they were previously in modern times.

This will have to be changed. Under the heading of *diplomatic* efforts we must increase resources and improve capabilities of preventive political action on different issues and in different parts of the world. Some of the possible avenues of approach have been indicated above. Under the heading of *development* should be grouped not only a reinforced commitment to the Millennium Development Goals, but also a stronger emphasis on all the issues of governance, democracy and reform throughout the world. And under the heading of *defense* we will have to accommodate the costs for the increases in manpower available not primarily for quick hard intervention operations, but for long-term stability operations as part of state-building efforts in volatile areas.

It is difficult to put numbers to the ambitions we must have in these fields, but it is certainly not an unreasonable conclusion of the new and more challenging international environment that we should seek to increase by at least 50 percent the share of GNP we spend on these combined 3D efforts for global stability. When this is done, spending on peace and security for our citizens is still likely to be below what it was during the height of the Cold War.

To do significantly less is to abdicate responsibility for the future stability of our world.

IV. A Pacific Asian Perspective

Coping with Threats to Human Security

Kazuo Ogura

The developments of the last fifteen years—dissolution of the East-West confrontation, the continuing politico-economic dichotomy between North and South, the wave of globalization of economic activities, and the spread of democracy—have brought new challenges to the fore which should redefine our Trilateral dialogue. These "global issues" include terrorism,[1] environmental destruction, drug trafficking, international crime, infectious diseases, refugee problems, and other issues broadly related to the concept of "human security."[2]

International dialogue, consultation, cooperation, and coordination are essential in dealing with these issues. One reason is that nowadays threats to "national" security cut across national boundaries. It is therefore essential to view those threats as threats to all mankind. The second reason is that

---

[1] Some people argue that, for policy purposes, one should distinguish terrorism motivated by clearly defined political objectives (such as independence for a certain region) from terrorism that appears to be driven by a desire for retribution or by strong ideological principles and where activities are more borderless, unlimited, and indiscriminate. Here we are focusing on the latter type of terrorism.

[2] For policy-oriented discussions, one can distinguish at least three different approaches to "human security." The first approach focuses mainly on protection from genocide or violation of human rights by civil war combatants or by dictatorial military regimes. The second approach is mainly concerned with protection from hunger and poverty. This approach assumes that the basic threat to human security in many parts of the world is the threat to human survival caused by deficiency and poverty. The third approach adopts a wider concept of human security, which includes protection from environmental degradation, terrorism, infectious diseases, international crime, and similar risks. These risks arise from politico-economic developments of recent decades and constitute a new type of threat to humanity in general.

Whichever approach one adopts, there seems to be a general consensus that the task for safeguarding human security requires both protection and empowerment of the people. Protection implies policies, resources, and institutions to protect people, while empowerment concerns the need for the people themselves to participate in developing human resources and politico-economic support.

sources of those threats, or sometimes the threats themselves, are interrelated. Therefore, in order to cope with those threats, we have to adopt a comprehensive approach (in contrast to a piecemeal or individual approach).[3] Thirdly, as we have witnessed in the case of infectious diseases or environmental degradation, we need prompt responses to some threats to human security. Slow reactions or loopholes in the system of protection can increase the cost of protection dramatically. Fourthly, these issues are often closely related to international business risks and therefore will affect, directly or indirectly, the activities of multinational corporations.

In order to cope effectively with these challenges that face us, at least three issues must be seriously considered. One is the problem of the roles of nation-states and international organizations in assuring legitimacy for international actions. The second is the question of cost sharing. How are the costs of supplying the public goods and services needed to secure human security to be covered? Third is the issue of public support. How can we mobilize domestic political will in each country for international endeavors to protect human security? These three problems are interrelated. Issues of principle and mechanism are related to the question of legitimacy, which is associated with the problem of mobilizing political support.

National Authorities, International Organizations, and the Legitimacy of International Actions

It is fashionable in Europe (and to a slightly lesser degree in the United States and Japan) to talk about borderless economies and the redefinition of nation-states. Yet in many parts of the world, national authorities are preoccupied with the problem of fostering or mobilizing popular sentiment for national unity and integrity. Nation-building is now in progress, and in some cases survival of the nation itself is at stake. We should not ignore the plea of many developing nations that global issues, however global their implications, should be addressed with the consent of nation-states and be based on cooperation and collaboration among them.

The issue of the roles of nation-states is closely related to the legitimacy of international actions to safeguard human security. In places where the security of each individual is seen as closely related to national security, as in the United States today involving protection from terrorist attacks, international action led by that nation-state looks quite legitimate as it is seen as directly related to national survival. In such a case, the legitimacy

---

[3] For example, HIV and food shortages are interrelated in some HIV-infected areas. Also, infectious diseases have made peacekeeping operations more difficult to carry out in affected areas.

of international actions can be determined by the particular national authority.[4]

In other places, even though the global threat to human security from terrorism is well recognized, national survival is not seen as at stake. In these cases, the legitimacy of international actions tends to be viewed as determined by international consensus. We should recognize more deeply that international consensus-building, and each nation's commitment to international legal and political principles, are essential for safeguarding human security.[5]

One tends to assume that decisions in or by the UN give legitimacy to international actions. This assumption is based upon another assumption, that the decisions of the UN are the manifest expression of the consent of nation-states which are members of the organization. We have, however, to distinguish between two aspects of the UN's role. One is legal, the other political. In the present globalized international context, the UN's decisions should perhaps be considered important more as a political expression of international opinion than the legal consent of member-states.

An important question we have to ask ourselves concerns the legitimacy of the UN itself. The UN has at least two problems in this respect. One relates to effectiveness or efficiency. The second is the degree of proper political representativeness. How we cope with these problems will affect the legitimacy of the UN in dealing with human security issues.

There is also the question of the roles of regional or ad hoc international groups or fora. Coalitions among those willing to take an initiative, such as the mechanism created by six countries to discuss the problems on the Korean Peninsula (with its primary focus on the nuclear proliferation issue), can be considered a new type of mechanism for international action to protect both national and human security.

Finally, what about the roles of NGOs and humanitarian aid agencies? Most people seem to agree that we have to rely more upon the international

---

[4] Nowadays one often hears the expression "American unilateralism." We should keep in mind that a nation is likely to have a unilateral tendency when its own survival is at stake and it has sufficient power to safeguard itself without particular assistance from others. The United States, as a superpower, can afford "unilateralism."

[5] From this standpoint, the Kyoto Protocol on global warming, the ban on certain types of landmines, establishment of the international criminal court, and ratification of the UN human rights conventions should be viewed as part of joint global efforts to protect human security. On the other hand, from the standpoint of national security, a few nations think that some international measures for protecting human rights run counter to their national security needs.

activities of NGOs, particularly in the area of human security. However, we must consider here the growing difficulties faced by international humanitarian agencies. This is related to the legitimacy of humanitarian activities and the concept of neutrality. Indeed, one of the most serious problems in promoting international efforts to protect human security is the steadily declining acceptance of the international norm that humanitarian aid should be placed above any politico-military conflicts, and that as long as the aid agency stays neutral, the aid agency should be immune to military attacks.

Today, such a notion of neutrality has been thrown into doubt. And in some internal conflicts or terrorist activities, it is practically difficult for the humanitarian aid agencies to stay neutral, which may incur the danger of attack.[6] This threatens to become a vicious circle. Actual or potential terrorist attacks create the need for humanitarian agencies to be protected by military force, which invites the threat of terrorist attacks even more.[7]

Sharing the Costs
The second problem concerns sharing the costs or burden to protect human security. How should we think about this sharing? How is it to be accomplished?

One practical line of thought is to ask those who benefit most from the expenditure to bear most of the expense. Joseph Nye provides food for thought in this regard in comments about organizing internationally against terrorism. "Even when there is broad acceptance of the general nature of a public good, there can be conflicts over its production....When there are many small participants, most fear that they will not reap benefits in proportion to the costs they pay, and the public good is difficult to produce. One of the virtues of a situation of unequal power like British naval preeminence in the 19th century, or American preeminence today, is that the largest country has an incentive to take the lead in suppressing piracy or terrorism because it knows it will gain a good part of the benefits."[8]

---

[6] The following fact eloquently reveals the difficulty of the matter: between 1942 and 1990, the Red Cross counted 15 victims among its officials. In the short span of six years after 1992, the number was 18.

[7] If the use of military power by national authorities to eradicate terrorism involves (predictable) civilian casualties, its legitimacy should be examined, among other factors, in relation to the repercussions on international humanitarian activities.

[8] Joseph S. Nye, Jr., "A North American Perspective" in Joseph S. Nye, Jr., Yukio Satoh, and Paul Wilkinson, *Addressing the New International Terrorism: Prevention, Intervention and Multilateral Cooperation* (The Trilateral Commission, 2003), p. 9.

This idea is not far from the practice which has more or less been implemented for UN peacekeeping operations. Those who are willing to shoulder the responsibility are supposed to bear the financial burden. This can be regarded as an application of the principle that those who benefit most should pay most. The problem which arises today is the gap between the willingness (or ambition) to shoulder responsibility and the financial capacity to pay. The U.S. deficits and the economic difficulties of some European countries are relevant in this light as well as in the light of risks to the world economy.[9]

The question of poverty should also be considered in this context.[10] The argument that poverty is sometimes the root cause of terrorism, infectious disease or drug trafficking should not be interpreted as a political excuse for the poor nations to avoid making contributions to international efforts to protect human security. The basic question is the economic (and political) cost-benefit calculation. If financial assistance to eradicate poverty in poor nations can raise their welfare and make them more capable, more conscious, and more willing to pay for the needed international cooperation (whether or not poverty is the root cause of the threat to human security), such assistance may be more important than direct financial contributions by rich nations to combat a particular threat against human security.[11]

In addition, we have to examine the need for speedy responses and readiness. For some threats to human security, such as infectious diseases, the most difficult aspect of the policy response is not necessarily the amount of financial resources, but the speed with which the problem is addressed. The example of Vietnam, which successfully coped with SARS, seems to indicate that what is at stake is the political will of the nation and international support for such national determination.

---

[9] There is a reverse type of gap in some other countries. Capacity to pay does exist but there is a lack of political will to shoulder international responsibility, mainly due to historical reasons. How to encourage these nations to be more forthcoming in this respect may be a task for the Trilateral dialogue.

[10] Many nations outside Europe, North America, and Japan refer to the importance of dealing with poverty not only due to the economic reality of poverty in the Third World but also due to the sense of injustice and the sentiment of impotence or helplessness which seems to have increased in some parts of the Third World as the wave of globalization spreads.

[11] In this connection, we must reflect further upon the balance of financial resources spent for national security and for human security in developing countries. Many developing countries still spend heavily on international arms transactions.

Mobilizing Public Support

The third and most difficult problem is how to mobilize public support for international actions to safeguard human security. Though this question is closely related to the problem of legitimacy, the problems are not identical. Even if legitimacy is more or less established by a sovereign state or states, this does not necessarily mean that the national authorities can automatically mobilize the political support of their people for international action, particularly military action.

There appears to be a (sometimes political and sometimes legal) threshold that is, for some countries, difficult to cross to arrive at national consensus for military action. On the legal aspect, recourse to military action is permitted under the UN Charter only in the case of self-defense. It is generally recognized that military action should meet two conditions: (1) it should be a response to an armed attack; and (2) it should observe the principles of necessity, proportionality and immediacy.

There is, however, a more serious problem with regard to the political threshold. Military intervention inevitably presupposes the risk of casualties to the nation's citizens. Military action on another nation's territory also may involve foreign civilian casualties, which may undermine the legitimacy of military intervention and create a domestic backlash against the military action. Taking into consideration the above-mentioned complexities, there is an effort to create "objective" criteria to be applied for international intervention.[12] Such an effort may be useful for clarifying some misgivings about international actions and for mobilizing domestic and international support for certain actions.

However, we should ask ourselves a more fundamental question. If international action or intervention includes the enforcement of measures by military intervention, we should ask whether an exercise which presupposes the use of military force should be encouraged at all. In other words, we should perhaps concentrate our efforts more on working out

---

[12] There is also an argument for developing a common definition of "threats." However, "threats" have both objective and subjective elements. Even if we succeed in developing a common objective concept of "threats," it does not necessarily lead to a consensus for particular international actions, since subjective sentiment about the "threats" varies from one nation or area to another. In this regard, it may be necessary to distinguish several types of threats to human security. For instance, international terrorism is related more to a sense of injustice and humiliation than to economic deficiencies. Other threats to human security, such as environmental pollution, drug trafficking or infectious disease, are more directly related to poverty.

the modalities with which military intervention be avoided at any cost. Under the present circumstances, sovereign nations can kill (by national or international military operations) unarmed civilians in the name of self-defense. Any effort to work out criteria which justify the use of military force by nation-states may end up redefining the (individual and collective) concept of "self-defense." Here, we have to recognize the differences of historical experience in different countries and regions of the world— differences which are essential elements of their political landscapes.

In more practical terms, this question finally boils down, in both the domestic and international arenas, to the question of political responsibility for actions. In the national sphere, it is quite clear that the head of government ultimately shoulders the political responsibility. In the international sphere, however, the place or person on which the ultimate political responsibility rests is unclear.

Therefore, what appears to be most important in practical terms is to share such responsibility. In this connection, we have to remind ourselves that economic development and the spread of democracy in the Third World have enhanced the legitimate right and aspiration of some emerging countries to participate more fully in international decision-making on trade, finance and security issues. The present system has not so far fully accommodated such aspirations. Consequently, many opinion leaders in India, Brazil and some other parts of the world have recourse to worldwide citizens' movements to have an impact, over the heads of national authorities, on the established international politico-economic framework.

If the citizens' vague sense of disenchantment (felt in the areas where globalization has increased the income gap) is mobilized for the benefit of some international political movement, the present system's legitimacy may be questioned even more, not only by non-governmental or citizens' groups, but also by some nation-states that want to challenge the present international system.

In the United States, Europe, and Japan, there is a tendency to see only the negative aspects of worldwide citizens' movements frequently associated with anti-globalization. However, there are some positive elements that we have to take into account. One is the role played by some movements in the developing world to heighten public consciousness of the need to adjust to the rapidly changing economic and political environment in the world. The second positive aspect is that the appeal of these movements (on an international scale) has reminded us of the need to consider the ethical and moral aspect (the problem of social justice) in the process of globalization.

In any event, states or governments can no longer maintain their quasi-monopoly over human (and even national) security issues. People themselves should shoulder more responsibilities in securing human security. The key to safeguarding human security rests in the hands of citizens. The ultimate success of international intervention depends on the political will of the people of the country or area where international actions have been taken. In this sense, the dialogue between citizens of the "intervening" and "intervened" sides is an essential part of assuring a durable political map for protecting human security.

*   *   *

Our Trilateral dialogue has, until now, more or less been confined to government or parliamentary leaders, businessmen, and public intellectuals such as journalists or academics. However, we should redefine this dialogue. We need to encourage dialogue including minority groups, labor unions, citizens' groups and NGOs, to encourage them to share a sense of responsibility in trying to resolve global issues.[13]

---

[13] In this regard, we have to reflect upon the "Chinese problem." If we expand, in some form, the Trilateral partnership to include China, there are historical problems for the West and Japan.

There is also the more imminent problem of Asian participation in world politics. One recalls in this connection a 2001 report to the Trilateral Commission entitled *East Asia and the International System*, the report of a special study group. "There is virtually no global problem that can be managed, much less resolved, without the participation of the major East Asian countries," the report notes. "Despite this, the countries of the region have not been major actors in shaping the institutions and rules of the international system." (p. 1) How to fill the gap between (potential) Asian politico-economic power and Asia's meaningful participation in international affairs, and between Asia's impact on the world and Asia's willingness to carry out international responsibilities, remains a task before the Trilateral Commission.